Welcome...

"The miniature world is one we can't see with the naked eye, so being able to view and capture it is an incredibly satisfying experience. I can still vividly recall what it was like trying close-up photography with a dedicated macro lens for the first time, even though more years than I care to remember have passed since that day! I was trying to capture creative flower images in the garden and when looking through the viewfinder, couldn't believe how magnified and detailed the small portion of the subject appeared. Wonder soon turned to frustration as I also discovered the many challenges that macro photography presents, from limited depth-of-field to image composition and lighting. However, persistence and experimentation eventually paid off and I was able to successfully capture some beautiful images. If you've developed an interest in macro photography, then *The Essential Guide to Close-up Photography* offers expert advice, creative ideas and essential techniques to help you master your photo skills and capture stunning close-up results. All manner of subjects are covered, from insects to flowers to everyday items you'll find around the home, so you won't be short of options. Enjoy your close encounters! All the best!"

DANIEL LEZANO, EDITOR

Meet our close-up experts

All our portrait experts are regular contributors to *Digital SLR Photography* magazine. For further advice and inspiration to help you improve your photo skills, pick up the latest issue, available on the second Tuesday of every month. For more information, visit: www.digitalslrphoto.com

ROSS HODDINOTT
Ross is an award-winning photographer with many years of experience and is the author of several books dedicated to macro photography.

DANIEL LEZANO
An enthusiast photographer for over 25 years, Daniel is an avid fan of macro photography, with a preference for shooting flowers and other natural subjects.

CAROLINE WILKINSON
A keen enthusiast photographer for several years, Caroline merges her in-depth knowledge of Photoshop with her creative camera skills to add extra impact to her pictures.

LEE FROST
A pro for two decades, Lee Frost's one of the best-known names in the UK photography business, with 20 books to his name and worldwide image sales.

The Essential Guide to Close-up Photography

Produced by *Digital SLR Photography* at:
6 Swan Court, Cygnet Park,
Peterborough, Cambs PE7 8GX
Phone: 01733 567401. Fax 01733 352650
Email: enquiries@digitalslrphoto.com
Online: www.digitalslrphoto.com

Editorial
To contact editorial phone: 01733 567401
Editor **Daniel Lezano**
daniel_lezano@dennis.co.uk
Art Editor **Luke Marsh**
luke_marsh@dennis.co.uk
Deputy Editor **Caroline Wilkinson**
caroline_wilkinson@dennis.co.uk
Features Writer **Jordan Butters**
jordan_butters@dennis.co.uk
Designer **Luke Medler**
luke_medler@dennis.co.uk
Editorial Co-ordinator **Jo Lezano**
jo_lezano@dennis.co.uk

Editorial contributors:
Ross Hoddinott, Lee Frost, Luoana Negut, Sailesh Patel,
Helen Sotiriadis, Andreas Stridsberg & Donna Willingham

Advertising & Production
Display & Classified Sales: 020 7907 6651
Group Advertising Manager
Alex Skinner
alex_skinner@dennis.co.uk
Sales Executive **Peter Smith**
peter_smith@dennis.co.uk
Production Controller **Daniel Stark**
daniel_stark@dennis.co.uk
Digital Production Manager **Nicky Baker**
nicky_baker@dennis.co.uk

Management
MAGBOOK PUBLISHER **DHARMESH MISTRY**
OPERATIONS DIRECTOR **ROBIN RYAN**
MD OF ADVERTISING **JULIAN LLOYD-EVANS**
NEWSTRADE DIRECTOR **DAVID BARKER**
COMMERCIAL & RETAIL DIRECTOR **MARTIN BELSON**
PUBLISHING DIRECTOR **JOHN GAREWAL**
CHIEF OPERATING OFFICER **BRETT REYNOLDS**
GROUP FINANCE DIRECTOR **IAN LEGGETT**
CHIEF EXECUTIVE **JAMES TYE**
CHAIRMAN **FELIX DENNIS**

CONTENTS

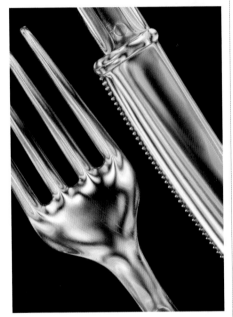

6 Introduction to macro
Everything you need to get started, including the kit, the focusing skills and the lighting.

27 Understanding the basics
From apertures and lighting to metering and composition, we guide you through the details to ensure close-up perfection.

44 Understanding macro kit
The right kit is essential for successful close-up shots. Here we cover all your options – macro lenses, close-up filters, extension tubes and reversing your lens.

54 Wild flowers
Shooting close-ups of nature's finest requires understanding of the right kit to use, how to 'garden' and creating a shallow depth-of-field.

70 Insects
Getting great shots of insects is a challenge – lighting and movement create problems that you need to learn how to overcome. Our tips and tricks will help you get great results.

87 Indoor techniques
Inspiring photo projects to keep you entertained at home.

131 Close-up equipment
You know how to capture close-ups and the type of kit you need, your next decision is what gear you should actually buy. Our tests to suit all budgets will make the decision easy.

TURN TO PAGE 130 TO FIND OUT ABOUT OUR FANTASTIC SUBSCRIPTION OFFERS

Transform your view of the world...

Look around and you'll see potential close-up shots everywhere. Objects that you wouldn't normally consider to have any photogenic merit look very different at close range. Sometimes the possibilities aren't obvious until you peer through your viewfinder, so don't dismiss anything until you've had a closer look

THERE IS NO BETTER place to begin than at home, especially when the UK weather hampers your plans to shoot outdoors. Your kitchen will be full of potential. There are all sorts of pots, pans and cooking implements that suit a close-up approach. The holes in a colander look abstract in close-up, or maybe take a frame-filling shot of a whisk. Try using a large aperture of f/2.8 or f/4 to create a shallow depth-of-field to produce an arty-looking result. Cutlery is also well-suited to being shot close-up, especially the curves and prongs of a fork. A +4 close-up filter, or extension tube, will allow you to get sufficiently near. A sheet of white card can provide a nice, simple backdrop for objects of this type and size. Place the card on a tabletop, lit by a window – this should provide enough ambient light to work with. To diffuse (soften) the light, hang a net curtain or some muslin across the window.

While you're in the kitchen, don't overlook the picture potential of food. Fruit and vegetables can look very striking close-up. Try slicing a kiwi or orange and backlighting the segments using a lightbox. Slice a red cabbage in half and you'll be surprised at the patterns revealed and, being a comparatively large subject, it should be possible to capture a frame-filling result by using the long end of a standard zoom. However, remember to position the camera parallel to the subject to maximise the available depth-of-field. Sweets are another good subject to snap, producing colourful, fun images.

You will find similarly photogenic objects in other rooms. Have a closer look at the electrical appliances in your living room. The styling and design of televisions, speaker grilles and computers lend themselves to being photographed. If you have a broken electrical device that you are about to throw out, carefully have a look inside before you do so. The internal workings and circuitry will look interesting close-up. Look for miniature detail that can be isolated. You may need a relatively high level of magnification to do this, so depth-of-field will be severely limited. A tripod will provide stability and also help you fine-tune composition.

Moving upstairs, have a look in the kids' bedrooms. Colourful building bricks, jigsaws, crayons and pencils are among the objects that can look abstract and striking. The key to photographing this type of object well is to be creative with your arrangement – for example, place felt-tip pens in a symmetrical formation. However, to ensure you record colours faithfully, remember to match your digital SLR's White Balance setting with the light source. For instance, the colour temperature of a household light bulb is typically 2800-3400K (Kelvin), meaning that it is warmer than the natural light filtering in through a window. Therefore, if you are using this type of artificial household light to illuminate your subject, it will create a warm, orange-looking colour cast if not corrected. To compensate, select your camera's tungsten or fluorescent White Balance preset, or manually dial in an appropriate setting.

Don't overlook fabrics and textiles either. A knitted jumper, ball of wool or the repetition of fabric weave can look intriguing through a close-up attachment, as it will help emphasise their texture and form.

While this will hopefully give you a few ideas to whet your appetite, you will soon think of many more when you begin looking around for potential subjects. Great results are possible even with basic equipment, and when you've finished taking pictures indoors, you can begin exploring the endless possibilities outside...

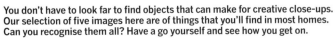

You don't have to look far to find objects that can make for creative close-ups. Our selection of five images here are of things that you'll find in most homes. Can you recognise them all? Have a go yourself and see how you get on.

Flowers

The beauty and symmetry of flowers are perfect for trying out macro photography – here are our top tips and advice to pull it off

FLOWERS ARE A FAVOURITE close-up subject. Not only do they create vibrant and interesting images, but they are also easily accessible to all. Whether you're photographing wild flowers like foxgloves, snowdrops and poppies, or cultivated species like lilies, orchids and tulips, the approach and technique required are generally the same.

Weather is a key consideration. Still days are best as flowers will sway in windy weather, making it nearly impossible to focus and compose images precisely. If you have no choice but to shoot in windy conditions, try steadying flowers using a clamp or windbreak. Overcast light is well-suited to flower photography, as the lower levels of contrast will allow you to faithfully capture colour and fine detail. A polarising filter can remove glare from reflective petals or foliage, helping restore natural colour saturation. Early morning and late evening light is warm and attractive and will complement flowers. Backlighting your subject will create atmospheric results, highlighting the translucency of petals and leaves and creating attractive rim lights around your subject. If you have no choice but to shoot in the middle part of the day – when the overhead position of the sun results in quite harsh, high-contrast light – keep a reflector close to hand. This will enable you to 'fill' dark shadow areas by bouncing light onto your subject.

When photographing flowers, a shallow depth-of-field will often create the most artistic-looking results. Opt for your lens's maximum aperture – normally f/2.8 or f/4 – and focus on a key area of interest or detail;

for example, the flower's stamens or the tip of a petal. With depth-of-field being so shallow, everything but your focal point will drift attractively out of focus, directing the eye to your chosen point.

Pay close attention to the subject's background. Simplicity is key. Normally, a nicely diffused, out-of-focus backdrop – free of mess, clutter or distracting elements – is best. To create a flattering background, only photograph flowers that you can easily isolate from their surroundings. Look for flowers taller than the ones around it, or which are a good distance from the background. Remove distracting grasses or twigs using scissors or flatten by hand. If possible, position yourself so that other out-of-focus flowers form the background, creating a pleasing wash of colour.

Of course, you don't have to photograph flowers outdoors. You can bring flowers in from your garden, or pop to a local florist for a handful of blooms. Shooting indoors allows you more control over lighting and background colour. You can position sheets of coloured card or fabric behind your set-up to form a simple contrasting background. Window light is a great form of illumination, so place your flower on a table where it will be bathed in natural light. The light can be diffused if necessary by hanging muslin over the window. By shooting indoors, you can capture great floral close-ups whatever the weather.

Finally, remember to only photograph pristine subjects – in close-up, even the smallest imperfection will be highlighted.

Flowers: creative ideas

Tiny water droplets add interest, sparkle and scale to flower and plant photographs, so head outside after rainfall or a dewy morning or, better still, create your own water droplets using a spray bottle. Position your camera parallel to the subject and select a small aperture to generate a generous depth-of-field. Droplets hanging down from petals, stems and leaves will act like tiny fisheye lenses, projecting an inverted image – employ a high magnification, close to 1:1 life-size, to capture the effect well.

Set yourself a garden project

In close-up, even the most ordinary, everyday objects can be transformed into a visual masterpiece. The trick is to teach yourself to view the world around you differently. A macro lens or close-up attachment allows you to isolate small areas of interest, so instead of looking at objects in their entirety, look closer for miniature detail and texture. Set yourself the task to go out into your own back garden and capture three great close-ups within an hour. It's a great discipline, making you look at familiar subjects in a completely new way. Wander around your garden and see what you can find. Rusty chains or padlocks, old keyholes, bolts, machinery, peeling paint, lichen, mossy stones, frogs and snails, and spider's webs are just a small example of the things you might find and which suit being photographed close-up. The way you light and arrange your subject can have a dramatic effect on the end result. Also, experiment with your viewpoints and the level of magnification. Once you start seeing in close-up, you will be surprised at the results you achieve.

ISTOCK PHOTO

HELEN DIXON

Create a floral triptych

So, having captured a number of flower-themed close-ups, what are you going to do with them? There is no point leaving them hidden on your computer's hard drive. Why not submit them to the *Showcase* pages of *Digital SLR Photography* magazine and try to get them published? Or you could print them on paper or canvas, and have them brighten up your wall space. Better still, why not create a stylish triptych to hang in your home or office?

A triptych is a collection of three related images that effectively work together to make a 'full' image, just like these above. Flowers are perfectly suited to this treatment. Creating one is very easily done using Photoshop or other photo-editing software.

Get the most from your macro still-lifes

Your home is the best place to start when it comes to finding subjects for still-lifes – even the most mundane items can be viewed for their beauty once you isolate small details. Train your eye to find them...

YOU DON'T HAVE to travel far to capture great still-life images. The average household is full of objects with great picture potential. When photographing still-life images, the photographer has complete control over every aspect of capture. Therefore, it is a great way to hone your compositional, lighting and exposure skills.

With still-life photography, you have to 'make' the picture before you can take it. Imagination is important – try to avoid the clichéd 'bowl of fruit' or 'vase of flowers' unless you have a different take on the idea. Potentially, even the most mundane, everyday objects can create striking photographs. Have a wander around your home. Cutlery, stationery, work tools, bottles and jars, sweets and toys all have potential – either photographed in isolation or combined with another object. You don't need an elaborate studio set-up – a modest tabletop with a couple of lamps or a flashgun will often suffice. When using artificial light, a photographer can carefully control its direction and quantity to create just the effect desired. However, if you are new to still-life photography, you might find it easier simply to use ambient light to begin with. If you are using household light, be aware that tungsten light has a warmer colour temperature than daylight. Set your White Balance to its Tungsten preset, or you'll notice images will suffer from a muddy, warm colour cast.

Contrast, colour, shapes, lines and form are all important ingredients to still-life photography. While colour will usually work best, don't overlook the possibilities of converting images to mono. Black & white can convey feelings of nostalgia, well-suited to some still-life subjects. Background is important, too. The right backdrop will help the subject stand out, while the wrong one will only hide it. Keep it simple and complementary.

Try capturing water droplets

Why not create a fantastic water abstract by photographing a droplet as it strikes the water's surface? Suspend a plastic bag, filled with water, 15-30cm above a black or glass dish on a tabletop and position your camera on a tripod in front of the set-up – a macro lens upwards of 90mm is best, allowing you to work further away to reduce the chances of your gear getting splashed. For best results, position your flash off-camera. Try placing it to the right of where your drop will fall and facing towards the background. The flash will bounce off the background, creating colour and a nice reflection. Select a small aperture of around f/16 to generate a good depth-of-field and set your shutter speed to the camera's flash sync speed. Set the flash to a 1/64 or 1/32 power setting – shortening the flash duration and generating a fast enough shutter speed to perfectly suspend the water's movement. Now, make a tiny hole in the bag using a pin. To aid focusing, briefly hold a pen or pencil in the water exactly at the point where the water is falling, and manually focus on this point. You're ready to take photos. Normally it's best to keep the room lights off. Be prepared to shoot lots of shots to get just one perfectly timed result. Experiment with different coloured backdrops and liquids – milk as well as water can create interesting results. For a full step-by-step guide to shooting water droplets, see page 128.

Set yourself a still-life project

Shooting close-up provides an abstract view of your subject. You can reveal easily overlooked detail, colour, symmetry, texture and repeating shapes, and isolate it in such a way that you create an eye-catching image. The subject matter doesn't even have to be recognisable – it is purely art. All kinds of household objects suit being captured this way – paper clips and pins, textiles, kitchen utensils and colourful sweets. To hone your creative eye, challenge yourself to capture at least one stunning close-up image in each room of your house. At first, you may struggle to identify suitable subjects, but once you get your eye trained, you will be surprised at how many things look striking close-up. If you have a lightbox from your days of shooting film, use it as a light source – it's ideal for illuminating small objects or backlighting transparent subjects.

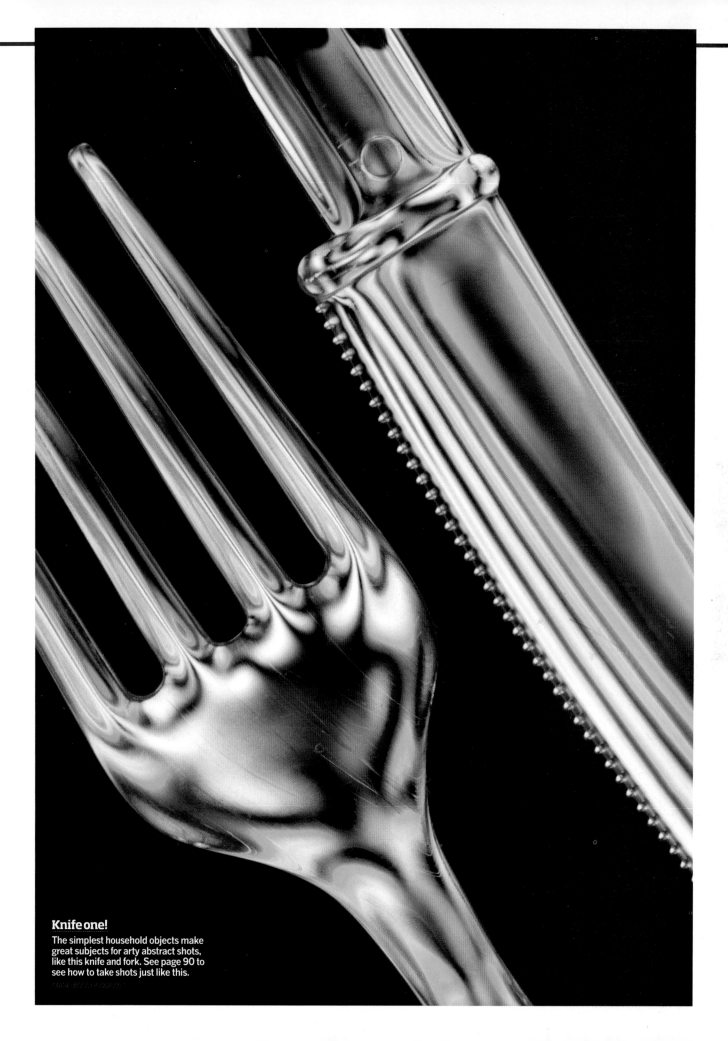

Knife one!

The simplest household objects make
great subjects for arty abstract shots,
like this knife and fork. See page 90 to
see how to take shots just like this.

Insects

Bugs are a macro photographer's favourite – here's how to make the most of their weird and wonderful characteristics

INSECTS UNDOUBTEDLY make great close-up subjects. Armed with your macro lens or close-up attachment, you can capture amazing frame-filling shots of alien-like bugs, with disproportionate eyes, large mandibles and long antennae.

Insects can be found almost anywhere, from your back garden to local parks, woodlands, wetlands and heathlands. Visit suitable locations and search carefully. Look among vegetation, tall grasses, on garden flowers and along water margins or hedgerows for small, photogenic subjects like ladybirds, lacewings, beetles, grasshoppers, moths, butterflies and dragonflies. Early mornings and late evenings are best to shoot insects, with subjects generally being less active. The light's quality will also be better and the sun's lower position will allow you to be more creative with lighting – you could try backlighting or silhouetting your subject.

Having located a suitable subject, next consider exposure settings. Depth-of-field is your priority, so select aperture-priority or manual exposure mode. Normally it is best to opt for an aperture small enough to keep your subject sharp, yet still large enough to throw surrounding vegetation out of focus. An aperture in the region of f/8 or f/11 is normally a good starting point, but the amount of depth-of-field you require will greatly depend on the subject, the level of magnification and the result you wish to achieve. You often have to work quickly, as insects are likely to move or fly away at any time. Therefore, using a tripod is rarely practical so you will normally have to shoot handheld. To keep shutter speeds workably fast – upwards of 1/250sec ideally – increase the ISO rating to 400 or 800 when required.

Like any wild creature, insects can be challenging to get close to. Maximise your chances of success by moving into position slowly, avoid casting your shadow over a subject and be careful not to knock nearby grasses or leaves in case you frighten your bugs away. Focus manually – not only is this a more precise method of focusing when shooting close-ups, but the noise of some AF systems can disturb your subject. Ensure the point of focus is on the creature's eyes and quickly shoot a short burst of images to maximise your chances of capturing at least one pin-sharp result.

Creative ideas: insects

To capture really eye-catching close-ups of insects, compose creatively. Insects often suit being photographed from a side angle or from directly overhead – particularly butterflies and moths with wings outstretched. As a result of this, it is easy to get in the habit of always photographing insects in the same manner. You shouldn't be afraid to be bold with composition, though. Try adopting a low worm's-eye viewpoint instead, or maybe shoot head-on to place emphasis on your subject's eyes and head in order to capture quirky insect portraits. Opting for a more unusual angle will help your insect shots stand out.

Although frame-filling shots will often boast lots of impact, don't overlook capturing your subject so that it is smaller in the image space. By including some of your subject's surroundings, you can convey far more about the subject and its environment. Doing so can produce a more stimulating and visually interesting composition. Including a degree of negative space will also create an enhanced feeling of scale and highlight the creature's small size. For a more in-depth look at shooting insects, turn to page 70.

Bug in focus
Insect shots with plain
backgrounds work
much better than those
with a messy backdrop.
IMAGE: ROSS HODDINOTT

Understanding close-up photography

Beginners are often put off trying close-up photography due to its specialist reputation. However, it isn't as tricky as people think, and you'll be pleased to know you can use kit you already own. Our guide will arm you with the know-how to begin taking great close-up images of your own

Reproduction ratio

The reproduction ratio is a way of describing the actual size of the subject in relation to the size it appears on the sensor – not the size to which the image is subsequently enlarged on screen or when printed. For example, if an object 40mm wide appears 10mm wide on the sensor, it has a reproduction ratio of 1:4 – or quarter life-size. If that object appears 20mm in size, it has a ratio of 1:2 – or half life-size. If it appears the same size on the sensor as it is in reality, it is described as having a reproduction ratio of 1:1 – or life-size. This can also be expressed as a magnification factor, with 1x equating to 1:1 life-size. A lens will have its reproduction ratio listed among its specification. Some standard and telezooms include the word 'macro' in their title. However, it is worth noting that this is simply an indication that it has a closer minimum focusing distance than normal. In reality, they can't be classified as a true macro lens, but they often boast a handy reproduction ratio of 1:3 or 1:4.

Eighth life-size

Quarter life-size

Half life-size

Life-size

ROSS HODDINOTT

Close-up or macro – so what is the difference?

The terms 'close-up' and 'macro' are often used to describe the same type of image. However, there is actually a distinct difference between the two. Technically speaking, a 'close-up' is an image with a reproduction ratio ranging from 1:10 to just below life-size: while 'macro' is life-size to 10:1 life-size. Anything taken with a greater magnification than 10x life-size belongs to the specialist field of micro-photography! Photographers, books and magazines tend to use the word 'macro' loosely to describe practically any close-up image. While this might be technically incorrect, in truth, the distinction is academic; it is the quality of the image that really matters.

Depth-of-field

One difficulty of close-up photography is working with a very limited depth-of-field. The zone of sharpness, in front of and behind the point of focus – for any given f/stop – grows progressively shallower as the magnification increases. For example, when photographing a flower, its stamens may be pin-sharp, but the petals in front and behind may be out of focus. Moving further away from the subject creates more depth-of-field, but this rather defeats the object. Instead, the solution is to use a smaller aperture (higher f/number), as this widens depth-of-field. As a result, the light reaching the sensor will be reduced so, to compensate, the shutter speed has to be lengthened to maintain the correct exposure. Unfortunately, a slower shutter speed raises the chances of camera shake. If the subject is static, the problem is easily remedied by using a tripod to support the camera. However, if the subject is moving or is wind-blown, the resulting shutter speed may not be fast enough to freeze movement. In situations like this, select a faster ISO rating or consider using a burst of flash. A good understanding of depth-of-field is important when shooting close-ups. The degree of back-to-front sharpness can greatly alter the appearance of the final image. Contrary to popular belief, lots of depth-of-field is not always desirable with close-ups, as it can bring distracting foreground and background elements in focus. Many photographers purposely opt for a narrow depth-of-field to isolate their subject and direct the viewer's eye to their chosen point of focus.

Sensor cropping

You are probably aware that the vast majority of digital SLRs have a cropped-type image-sensor, generally termed an APS-C sensor, meaning that they are smaller than the traditional 35mm film frame. This narrows the field-of-view and effectively multiplies the focal length of the lens, although the actual focal length doesn't change. The degree of multiplication depends on the size of the sensor, but with a crop-factor of 1.5x, for example, a 100mm lens effectively becomes 150mm. This can be a disadvantage in some areas of photography, such as landscapes, as wide-angle lenses lose their characteristic effects. However, for close-ups it is hugely beneficial in two ways. Firstly, the narrower angle-of-view can be used to provide a larger working distance from the subject as you can shoot from further away while maintaining the same level of magnification that would be achieved with a full-frame sensor – useful if you're shooting wildlife that is easily disturbed. Also, you will block less light from reaching the subject. Alternatively, a DSLR with an APS-C sensor can be used to increase the subject's size within the frame. This is because the sensor crop doesn't alter the minimum focusing distance, so its reproduction ratio is effectively extended.

Full-frame

Cropped

ROSS HODDINOTT

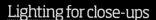

Lighting for close-ups

Natural light can be restricted when shooting close-ups. Often, this is due to the close proximity of the camera to the subject – with the photographer, camera or both casting a shadow across small subjects. This can be tricky to avoid, especially when using close-up attachments as the lens may be positioned only centimetres away. Sometimes the problem can be solved by simply altering the shooting position or by using a longer focal length to increase the subject-to-camera distance. However, if this isn't possible you may need to supplement the available light. For the most natural-looking results, reflect light back onto the subject using a reflector. The intensity of light can be altered by moving the reflector closer or further away, and by adjusting the angle. Compact, collapsible versions are cheap and an ideal accessory to keep in your kit bag. Alternatively, a piece of white card or tin foil can be used. If a reflector doesn't work, try using flash. However, flash from a hotshoe-mounted flashgun may well miss (or only partially illuminate) the subject, either passing overhead or being obstructed by the lens barrel. Therefore, position your flashgun off-camera, using an off-camera flash cord.

When you're making your first steps into close-up photography, we'd recommend you experiment with window light to begin with, as it's relatively easy to work with.

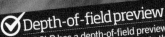

Depth-of-field preview
If your DSLR has a depth-of-field preview button, use it. It stops down the lens to the current aperture setting, so you can preview what will and what won't be in focus through the viewfinder. Works well with LiveView, too

PETER ADAMS

Essential kit for close-ups

Whether you're just starting out or taking your macro work to the next level, there are some bits of kit that are perfect for the job in hand...

TO CAPTURE good macro images, you need to be able to achieve a high level of magnification, beyond the capability of most standard lenses. In order to get close to small things, you either need a dedicated macro lens – optimised for close focusing – or an attachment that will convert your standard optic into a close focusing device. A dedicated macro lens is best, offering both quality and convenience, but being a specialist lens choice, these can be pricey. If you intend to take a lot of close-ups, it is well worth the investment and it will prove a good

addition to your kit bag. However, if you are just dabbling with macro at this stage – or need to work within a budget – a close-up filter or auto extension tube is the better and cheaper option.

There are also a few essential accessories you will require, several of which you will likely already have. The most important is a good tripod. The smallest movement is exaggerated in close-up, so whenever practical, use a support. A remote release will also prove useful, as will a small reflector – either bought or home-made.

Three ways to get close...

£350+

Macro lens

A true macro lens is capable of a reproduction ratio of 1:1 (life-size). Typically, they are prime, fixed focal lengths with a fast maximum aperture, ranging from 50mm to 200mm. Although – bar one or two – they're all capable of the same level of magnification, the actual focal length remains significant, helping determine the weight, size, cost and working distance.

Shorter macros from 50mm to 90mm are lighter and smaller, and tend to be cheaper. They don't provide such a large camera-to-subject distance, so for frame-filling shots, you'll need to get closer to the subject. This is fine for inanimate objects, but can prove a problem when shooting wildlife. A tele-macro, with a focal length upwards of 90mm, provides a larger working distance, reducing the risk of disturbing subjects. However, they are heavier, so you're more likely to need a tripod. Also, due to the narrower angle-of-view, they appear to produce a shallower depth-of-field, so focusing must be extra precise.

£50+

Auto extension tubes

A cut-price option is auto extension tubes. Basically, they are hollow tubes that fit between camera and lens. By doing so, they reduce the lens's minimum focusing distance, therefore increasing the level of magnification. As they are constructed without optics, they don't degrade the lens's optical quality, but they do reduce the amount of light entering the camera; the higher the magnification, the more light lost. Tubes are compact, light and – combined with a quality lens – capable of great results. Common lengths include 12mm, 25mm and 36mm – the wider the tube, the greater the extension. They are best combined with short prime focal lengths – in the region of 35mm to 100mm. Kenko is among the few brands to produce them. Non-auto versions are available cheaply – around £10. However, the lack of electronics means they disable many of the camera's key automatic functions, like certain exposure modes and focusing, so you need to do everything manually.

£10+

Close-up filters

Don't worry if you can't afford a macro lens or extension tube – this is the most affordable option. They are circular screw-in type filters, which – in simple terms – act like a magnifying glass. They provide a great introduction to close-up photography. They are light and do not affect the lens's automatic functions. Hoya, Kood, Micro Tech Labs, Nikon and Raynox are among the brands producing filters. Their magnification is measured in dioptres and they are available in a range of diameters and strengths, typically +1, +2, +3 and +4. The higher the number, the greater their magnification. +10 versions are also available, but their quality tends to be fairly low. They are best paired with short prime lengths, in the region of 50mm to 135mm. Close-up filters don't provide a large working distance, so be prepared to get close to your subject to capture frame-filling shots. They are also prone to spherical and chromatic aberration – image quality can be maximised by selecting an aperture no smaller than f/8.

Essential accessories

Reflector: A reflector is a 'must have' for close-up photography – invest in one if you're taking a lot of close-ups. A 30cm or 45cm reflector will more than suffice for much of the time. Its colour is important: white will provide a soft, diffused light; silver is more efficient, but can look harsh; while gold or sunfire will add warmth to close-ups. A cut-price alternative is to wrap foil around a piece of card.

Remote release: Even when a camera is tripod-mounted, physically depressing your camera's shutter release button can generate slight movement. At slower shutter speeds, this can soften picture quality and ruin a potentially brilliant image. Therefore – whenever practical – trigger the shutter remotely using either a corded or infrared remote. This maximises image sharpness – particularly in combination with your camera's mirror-lock facility.

Tripod: For pin-sharp close-ups, use a tripod whenever it's practical to do so. Look for one with good low-level capability. For example, Manfrotto's XPROB design allows the centre column to be positioned horizontally, the Gitzo Systematics lack a centre column altogether, while Giottos models with a 3D column are also perfectly suited to close-up work. The design and type of head you combine it with is very much down to personal taste. However, the precision of geared heads is well-suited to macro.

Plamp: The Wimberley Plamp is a ball & socket segmented arm with a clamp fixed at each end. One clamp fastens to one of the legs on your tripod, while the other can be used to hold an object. They are particularly handy for holding a reflector in place, but can also be used to hold your subject steady or in position – for example, a windblown flower or branch. A useful addition to your kit bag.

Right-angle finder: The introduction of LiveView and vari-angle monitors means right-angle finders are less popular now. They are L-shaped attachments that fit onto the camera's eyepiece to allow you to view and compose images by peering downwards, rather than horizontally, into the viewfinder. When shooting at low or ground level – which can be often with macro work – an angle finder allows you to compose images more comfortably.

Suggested macro outfits to suit every budget...

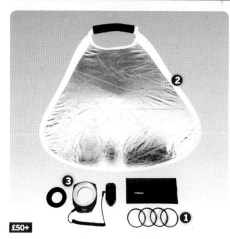

£50+

£300+

£700+

Getting started

You haven't tried shooting close-ups before, but want to give it a go. Therefore, you have a limited budget – there is no point spending too much at this stage. Although you can't justify a dedicated macro lens, you can still get close enough to most subjects by using an inexpensive close-up attachment. However, macro lenses don't provide a large working distance, so prioritise photographing inanimate subjects, like still-lifes, textures, patterns, flowers and plants, rather than small wildlife.

1) Close-up filters (£10+ depending on filter size): A +3 or +4 close-up will provide a good introduction to close-ups, converting your normal lens into a makeshift macro. Combining them will provide a greater level of magnification, but expect image quality to drop. Hoya produces a good range of quality filters.

2) Reflector (£10+): Although you could make your own by attaching kitchen foil to a sheet of card, buying a proper reflector is recommended, especially if you'll be using it often. They fold away and will easily slip into your camera bag. A sunlite/soft silver version will provide a nice natural light source. A 30cm reflector is large enough for small subjects.

3) LED ringflash (£30+): Provides soft, shadow-free lighting for close-ups at a fraction of the cost of a normal ringflash. You can control the output level of the LEDs, and either fire them or keep them on constant. A power pack attaches to the camera's hotshoe. Hama, Polaroid and Seagull are among the makers.

Getting experienced

You are hooked and want to take better close-ups. Therefore, it is time to invest a little more cash into your photography in order to buy kit that will allow you to capture superior image quality. A macro lens is still beyond your current budget, but auto extension tubes will provide sharper, crisper results compared to using dioptres. Camera-to-subject distance will still be short, but the addition of a good tripod to your set-up will allow you to widen the list of subjects you can shoot successfully.

1) Auto extension tubes (£50-£75): Unlike close-up filters, extension tubes don't degrade image quality. A 50mm f/1.8 is a good choice for use with tubes. Polaroid and Zeikos produce budget auto tubes.

2) Tripod (£100-£150): A tripod helps you fine-tune composition and enables you to place your point of focus more accurately. The Manfrotto 190XPROB is a good choice, with a centre column that can be placed horizontally and legs that can be splayed flat.

3) Ringflash adaptor (£80+): These convert a hotshoe-mounted flash into a ringflash. They lack the functionality of a dedicated ringflash, but are a good cut-price option. Try Rayflash or Orbis. Arguably offers little advantage over the cheaper LED ringflash for macro.

4) Plamp (£35): Not particularly expensive, but a useful gadget to keep in your gadget bag when shooting close-ups. Ideal for holding a reflector in place, for steadying a branch or flower stem, or for generally acting like an extra hand.

Getting serious

You've realised that close-ups are your thing. You're beginning to specialise in macro photography and are prepared to spend whatever it takes to ensure you have the right kit for the job. A dedicated macro lens is your priority. By allowing you to take close-ups from further away, it is possible to shoot any close-up subject, including timid insects. A dedicated macro flash is also on your list, together with a tripod head that will give you ultimate control and precision over composition and focusing.

1) 100mm macro lens (£400+): A sensible choice, giving a practical working distance, but short and light enough to use handheld when required. A lens with image stabilisation is beneficial for handheld work.

2) Tripod & head (£100+): You want to be able to make small, precise adjustments to composition quickly, without any movement when you tighten up controls. The geared design of the Manfrotto 410 is a popular choice.

3) Macro flash (£200+): LED ringlights and adaptors are good makeshift options, but a dedicated macro flash is best. They give you the most functionality and allow you to take well-lit close-ups in any conditions. Check units from Sigma, Canon, Nikon and Metz.

4) Right-angle finder (£40+): Unless your DSLR has a vari-angle screen, a right-angle finder is a great aid – when shooting flowers or amphibians from ground level, for example. Nikon and Canon both make right-angle finders but budget brands like Seagull are available, too.

If your budget can stretch to it...

Ring/macro flash

When natural light isn't enough, a dedicated macro ringflash is best for functionality and performance. It attaches to the front of the lens via an adaptor, producing a ring of light, enabling the flash to illuminate subjects in all directions. To prevent this type of light from being entirely shadowless

£200+

and flat, most allow ratio control so that the light from one side of the ring can be stronger than the other. They can be difficult to diffuse, though, and tend to produce doughnut-shaped reflections on shiny surfaces.

Auto reversing ring

Reversing rings allow a lens to be mounted back to front. Doing so generates a high level of extension, which enables the lens to focus much closer. The level of magnification achieved by reversing a lens is determined by focal length and the level of displacement, but can exceed twice

£250

life-size. Electronic lens mounts mean manual rings are far less popular, but there is a solution if you're a Canon user: the Novoflex EOS-Retro Adaptor (www.speedgraphic.co.uk) retains all the camera's auto functions.

The basics of close-ups

There are a number of things you'll need to think about when shooting macro to get the best possible results in any given situation…

CLOSE-UP PHOTOGRAPHY has a reputation for being fiddly and challenging, which deters some photographers from giving it a try. However, while it is true that working so close to your subject can present a few technical challenges, so long as you are armed with the knowledge and technique to overcome them, there is no reason why you shouldn't be capturing great close-ups straight away. The biggest issue close-up photographers face is achieving sufficient depth-of-field to keep their subject acceptably sharp. Depth-of-field grows progressively shallower at higher magnifications, so the zone of sharpness can be very shallow indeed. Therefore, your choice of aperture is hugely important, which is why aperture-priority and manual are the modes best suited to macro.

Simply opting for a high f/number, like f/16 or f/22, might seem like the obvious thing to do when shooting close-ups. However, every situation is different – some subjects will suit a large depth-of-field, others a shallow zone of sharpness; you have to decide. If you require your subject to be sharp throughout, a high f/number is the best option. Also, try to position your camera parallel to the subject itself to maximise depth-of-field. The main drawback of using a high f/number is that the corresponding shutter speed will be slower – increasing the risk of camera shake or subject movement – and foreground and background detail will also be more in focus, thus more of a distraction. A lower f/number creates a shallower depth-of-field. While this means you have to focus with greater precision, a shallow zone of focus throws the subject's surroundings attractively out of focus, placing more emphasis on the subject itself. The resulting shutter speed will also be quicker, making it possible to work handheld if necessary. Achieving just the right combination of acceptable depth-of-field and background blur is a tricky balance. If your camera has a depth-of-field preview button, use it to help preview how the image will look using the settings you've chosen – on some models, it is possible to do this in combination with LiveView. Another option is to simply shoot a series of images, taken at various f/stops, for later comparison.

Focusing is another key consideration. Cameras struggle to focus at such short distances and, along with shallow depth-of-field, means unsharp images are a real risk. Manual focus is typically the best option, allowing you to select and place your point of focus with great accuracy – an insect's eyes or the stamens of a flower, for example. When using a tripod, LiveView is a great focusing aid. Using the zoom button, you can magnify small, specific parts of the image in order to check critical sharpness and make very fine adjustments to focus.

At higher magnifications, the smallest movement appears exaggerated, so the risk of camera shake is increased, so keep a careful eye on shutter speed. A tripod is the best solution, but if you shoot handheld, use a shutter speed upwards of 1/200sec and switch on Image Stabilisation. Increasing the ISO rating is another good option.

> "Focusing manually will allow you to select and place your point of focus with great accuracy – an insect's eyes or the stamens of a flower, for example"

Close-up on light

Natural light

Light is a key ingredient to any photograph – and close-ups are no exception. The light's quality, colour, direction and contrast are all contributing factors. Light can help highlight, enhance or conceal the appearance of minute detail – front, side and backlighting each have their own individual qualities.

Front-lighting – when the subject facing the camera is directly lit – tends to produce quite even, shadowless light. It is good for emphasising colours, making them appear richer and more vibrant, but otherwise can create quite flat results, lacking contrast. Also, when working so close to the subject, it can be difficult to avoid casting your shadow over the subject when it's front-lit.

Side-lighting is normally better, highlighting form and defining shapes and edges – although to what degree will depend on the subject and the angle and intensity of the light. Strong side-lighting can create too much contrast, though. When contrast is too great, relieve shadows using a reflector or fill-flash.

Backlighting is the most difficult to manage, but can produce the most striking results. When the light source is behind the subject, it will highlight a subject's shape, form and fine detail – like the tiny hairs on a flower stem. Early morning and late evening are the best times of day to shoot backlit subjects, as the sun is low in the sky. Attach a lens hood to prevent flare and review your image's histogram regularly – backlighting can fool TTL metering into exposure error; apply exposure compensation if photographs are under- or overexposed. Backlighting is particularly well-suited to translucent subjects, like leaves and insect wings. Indoors, a lightbox can be used to create a

Get set for close-ups!

Quality
Select Raw mode. When shooting close-ups, you want to capture the best quality file possible, one that will capture the finest detail and widest range of tonal levels. Shooting in Raw will allow you to do this and, compared to JPEGs, they have a greater impunity to any changes you make during post-processing.

Exposure mode
Your priority is controlling and altering the amount of depth-of-field, so use aperture-priority (A/Av) or manual (M) mode. You can work most efficiently in aperture-priority – select the f/stop that gives the depth-of-field you require, and the camera automatically sets the corresponding shutter speed.

ISO rating
When practical, select the camera's lowest ISO rating to maximise image quality and capture fine detail. While a low ISO is fine when using a tripod or shooting static subjects, increase sensitivity for a faster shutter speed when working handheld or photographing wildlife or windblown vegetation, .

Focusing
Generally speaking, manual focus offers the most precision and control when photographing nearby objects. When using a tripod, activate LiveView. Zoom in to the area or point you wish to focus on and, in combination with manual focusing, you can place your point of focus with pinpoint accuracy.

HELEN DIXON

similar backlit effect. You could even go further and silhouette your subject. Contre-jour photography relies on simplicity. Opt for instantly recognisable subjects and contrast your subject against a warm, colourful sky. To create a silhouette, meter correctly for the brighter background.

Don't overlook overcast light either. Clouds act like a giant diffuser, softening the sun's intensity and producing flattering, low-contrast light. Bright, overcast light is particularly well-suited to close-ups of flora, allowing close-up photographers to capture fine detail and rich, saturated colours.

Artificial light
While photographers often favour natural illumination, light is often in short supply when working so close to the subject. It can be difficult to avoid your body or camera physically blocking the light due to your close proximity. In addition to this, a degree of light is naturally lost or absorbed at higher magnifications. A solution is to use reflected light, employing a reflector to bounce extra light onto the subject. However, when natural or reflected light isn't sufficient to freeze a subject's motion or capture fine detail and colour, try flash. The pop-up or hotshoe-

mounted flash may miss or only partly illuminate nearby objects due to its relatively high position, so a dedicated macro/ringflash is best. When using artificial light, the goal is still to produce results that appear natural. This can prove difficult when the flash is positioned so close to the subject, which is why diffusion is essential to prevent flashlight looking harsh and artificial. There are few diffusers available for ringflash units, so try making your own. The best option is to cut and fix rings of kitchen towel or paper to the flash ring. Doing so softens the light and creates more natural-looking results.

White Balance
Automatic White Balance (AWB) is reliable in the majority of situations. However, it can be fooled if the subject is predominantly one tone. In situations like this, it is better to select the most appropriate WB preset. If shooting in Raw, you can fine-tune colour temperature to taste during post-production.

Mirror lock-up
When using a tripod, select your camera's Mirror lock-up facility (if it has one). This raises the reflex mirror prior to firing the shutter. eliminating internal vibrations which can soften fine detail. When using the function, it takes two presses to take the picture: the first press locks up the mirror; the second takes the photo.

Checklist: The basics

✓ Think carefully about your choice of aperture before taking a shot. To generate a large depth-of-field and achieve a high level of sharpness throughout, opt for a high f/number (narrow aperture); to isolate your subject against a diffused, out-of-focus background, set a low f/number (wide aperture).

✓ Don't get lazy with focusing. Focus manually for greater precision. Better still, activate LiveView and zoom into your subject to check critical focus.

✓ Don't overestimate how still you can hold your camera – shooting images in close-up emphasises even the slightest of movements. Our advice? Use a tripod whenever possible for your macro shots, and prioritise a shutter speed fast enough to eliminate camera movement when shooting handheld.

✓ To help maximise the depth-of-field available to you, always try to keep your camera parallel to the subject.

✓ To maximise sharpness, employ a support, use your camera's mirror lock-up facility and trigger the shutter using a remote device – even pressing the shutter manually can introduce shake.

✓ Think carefully about how you position yourself in relation to the sun. When working in close proximity to the subject, be careful that your own shadow doesn't cast your subject into shade as it can frighten your subject away.

Essential skills you need to master close-ups

Shooting strong macro images comes down to good in-camera technique and strong composition. Taking control of focusing, depth-of-field and lighting will help you get the best possible results

Focusing

In close-up, the point of sharpest focus appears more pronounced through the viewfinder. However, just because it is easier to see doesn't mean it is easier to position! A good focusing technique is essential for close-ups – even the smallest error can prove disastrous to the final shot.

Depth-of-field is inherently shallow at high magnifications, meaning your point of focus needs to be placed with pinpoint accuracy. You might think that the best option would be to use autofocus. In practice, though, AF is rarely the best choice as it can struggle to lock on to nearby objects – particularly in low light or if the subject is low contrast – so AF tends to 'hunt' or 'search' for focus. It is normally easier, and more precise, to focus manually, so switch to manual focus (MF). Doing so allows you to place your focus on your chosen point – an insect's eyes or the flower stamen, for example.

If you are shooting handheld, it can be useful to prefocus your lens and then move slowly forward towards the subject, with camera to eye, until it is sharp through the viewfinder. If necessary, gently move back and forth, releasing the shutter when the subject is in sharpest focus. With the zone of sharpness being so narrow – maybe only a matter of millimetres – it is best to take a couple of frames to help ensure at least one bitingly sharp result.

A tripod is a great focusing aid – with the camera in a fixed position, it is far easier to focus. Better still, employ your camera's LiveView facility in combination with a tripod – this is undoubtedly the best technique for close-ups. No other technique allows you to place your point of focus with such accuracy. Again, focusing manually is generally the best method.

ISTOCK PHOTO

Reflectors

Reflectors are circular disks with either a white, silver or gold side that can be positioned near to the subject in order to bounce light onto the subject. Small collapsible versions are produced by the likes of Interfit and Lastolite, but card covered in tinfoil, or a mirror, can also do the job. They allow you to control the light and its direction, and ensure your subject isn't in shadow. You can alter the light's intensity by simply moving the reflector closer or further away. Unlike flash, you can see the effect of what you are doing instantly and adjust the reflector's position accordingly. Reflectors are perfect for relieving dark, harsh shadows and for giving small subjects extra illumination in shady or overcast conditions. They are a must-have accessory for close-up photographers working outdoors.

No reflector

With reflector

An eye for detail
Focus carefully and use a
wide aperture to ensure
only a specific area of the
scene is sharp.
IMAGE iSTOCK PHOTO

Make the most of ambient light

Light is a key ingredient to all photographs, and close-ups are no different. The light's colour, contrast and direction play an important role in enhancing or concealing the appearance of miniature detail. However, light can be in short supply when working in close proximity to your subject. When shooting close-ups, it is often impossible to avoid your body or camera physically blocking the light and casting your subject into shade due to your close shooting position. Also, quite a lot of light is naturally lost at higher magnifications – two stops at 1:1. Ideally, when working with natural light, choose scenarios where the subject is side- or backlit. Side-lighting can suit close-ups, as it will enhance surface texture and detail and give your images a three-dimensional feel. Beware strong side-lighting, though – shadows can be too exaggerated, resulting in too much contrast.

Backlighting, where the light source is behind the subject, can create fantastic results and will highlight shape, form and intricate detail. It is particularly well-suited to translucent subjects, like butterfly wings and leaves. Backlighting can fool TTL-metering systems into underexposing results, though, so keep an eye on the histogram and apply positive exposure compensation if required. Attach a lens hood, too, to reduce flare.

Of course, side- or backlighting may not always be possible or desirable. However, when the subject is lit from the front, it is often difficult not to obstruct the light's path. In instances like this, you may need to give the natural light a helping hand by using flash or a reflector. One of the biggest advantages of working in close-up is that photographers have far more control over their subject, their surroundings and – crucially – lighting. If the natural light needs supplementing, it is easy to do so. While the quality of light is best during dawn and dusk, close-up photographers can capture good images any time of day as they are able to manipulate the light more. The easiest way is with a small reflector. ➲

The beauty of cloud cover

As with most things artistic, there is no universal rule as to what constitutes the best light – much depends on your subject and creative intent. Photographers often obsess about light, but sometimes the best conditions are when it is dull. You don't always need strong or dramatic directional light to capture great shots. Overhead clouds act as giant diffusers, creating flattering, low-contrast light that will enable photographers to capture fine, intricate detail and record colour with greater accuracy. In fact, there are times when the best option is to cast your subject into shade as this eliminates unwanted shadows and lowers image contrast. However, when shooting in overcast light, shutter speeds will be longer, meaning subject and camera movement is a greater concern. Therefore, either increase your camera's ISO sensitivity to generate a workable fast shutter speed or only shoot static subjects when using a tripod.

Tripod choice

When working with close-ups, depth-of-field grows progressively shallower. Also, the smallest movements seem greatly exaggerated at high magnifications. As a result, achieving correctly composed and focused close-ups can prove difficult if shooting handheld. Though it isn't always practical to use a support, use a tripod whenever possible. While a monopod or beanbag can be suitable in certain situations, tripods offer an unrivalled level of stability. They virtually guarantee sharp, shake-free results and allow you to fine-tune your composition and place your point of focus – either through the viewfinder or via LiveView – with greater precision. Don't opt for a cheap, flimsy model – buy good, sturdy legs. Close-up photographers require certain functionality in a tripod, like the ability to shoot at low level. Look for a design where the legs can be spread low to the ground, particularly with a centre-column that can be split in half or tilted down to get the camera even lower. Giottos has a good range, or the popular manfrotto 190 and 055 models with a horizontal centre-colum option. Benbo's unusual, innovative tripod design is also perfectly suited to close-ups. Budget at least £100 for good legs.

Next, consider head type. A three-way pan & tilt design is a good option, while many close-up photographers favour a ball & socket head as they offer quick, easy movement. Buy a model with an appropriate load capacity for your kit. For static subjects, a geared head, like Manfrotto's 410 Junior head (above), is the perfect choice, allowing very fine, precise movements. Budget between £50-£140 for a good head. The leg/head combination you prefer can be a very subjective thing, and the combination you opt for greatly depends on the way you prefer working and personal taste. Therefore, always try before you buy where possible. ➡

ROSS HODDINOTT

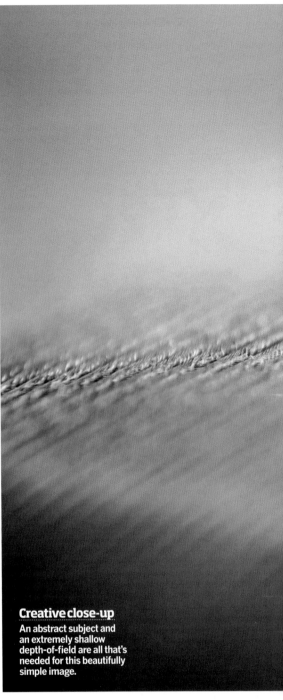

Creative close-up

An abstract subject and an extremely shallow depth-of-field are all that's needed for this beautifully simple image.

Q&A: Close-ups

Q My camera has a 'Macro' exposure mode. Is it worth using?
A Most digital SLRs and CSCs have a number of scene modes, developed to bias settings according to a specific type of subject. Basically, they are variations of the fully automatic Program (P) setting. By selecting the camera's 'Macro' mode, it will attempt to select the best f/stop and shutter speed combination to shoot close-up subjects. The camera will prioritise a high f/number in order to create a large depth-of-field to render close-up subjects in focus, while still providing a fast enough shutter to eliminate camera shake. While auto picture modes may seem hassle-free, in reality they offer very limited creative control and your camera can't predict the type of result you are after. Therefore, your best bet is to select aperture-priority mode, as this will allow you complete control over depth-of-field, and give you a much greater chance of getting the result you're after.

Q Can I shoot close-ups in windy weather?
A The smallest movement can seem hugely exaggerated in close-up, so wind can prove a major obstacle. Check the weather forecast and shoot close-ups when the wind speed doesn't exceed 10-14mph. However, this is the UK, so you can rarely rely on the weather! On windier days, select subjects growing in more sheltered areas, or position yourself – or a friend – to block the breeze with your body. Alternatively, erect a makeshift windbreak using clear polythene and garden canes. Another option is to use a clamp. A Wimberley Plamp is ideal. It is a flexible segmented arm with a clamp at both ends. Attach one end to a tripod leg, using the other to stabilise your subject.

Q Is it worth buying a right-angle finder?
A A right-angle finder is an L-shaped attachment that fits to the camera's eyepiece, allowing you to view and compose images by peering downwards, rather than horizontally,

into the viewfinder. They are useful when shooting close-ups from low or awkward angles. If you regularly shoot low-level, or suffer from back pain, then they are a good investment. However, LiveView makes it easy to compose images from awkward angles today, and if you own a model designed with a vari-angle LCD, you won't need one.

Q Should I trigger the shutter remotely when shooting close-ups?
A Much depends on the situation, but if you are shooting a static subject, and the camera is on a tripod, then yes – doing so will maximise image sharpness. Using a tripod doesn't completely guarantee image sharpness – physically depressing the shutter button can generate a small amount of movement that may soften image quality, particularly at slow shutter speeds. Although the effect is fairly minimal, even the tiniest vibration appears greatly magnified in close-up, so this is of particular

relevance to close-up photographers. It is good practice to always use a remote device or the camera's self-timer when practical to do so. Doing so allows you to trigger the shutter remotely without touching the camera.

Q When photographing shiny objects, how do I reduce reflections and hotspots?
A While flash diffusers and reflectors can help, to eliminate highlights altogether you need to diffuse the light. Try a light tent by Lastolite or Kaiser, or create your own with translucent acrylic, tracing paper or a white sheet draped over a frame. Place your object within your tent, positioning your camera so the lens enters the tent through the open front. Position at least two lamps, or off-camera flash units, outside the tent, either side of it. If hotspots still exist, adjust the lamps' positions. Also try shooting outdoors on an overcast day – cloud cover is a perfectly diffused natural light source. Polarising filters also reduce reflections.

Flash

When ambient light is insufficient for close-ups, flash is the answer. There are many advantages to using artificial light. Flash provides illumination when light levels are low, preventing the blurring effects of subject or camera movement. It allows a smaller aperture to be employed, creating a larger depth-of-field than would otherwise have been possible. Applied well, it will highlight fine detail and help create sharper results. It can be used to fill dark shadows, highlight the subject's shape and form, or to produce more intense colours. Quite simply, flash provides photo opportunities that wouldn't have existed otherwise.

Illuminating small subjects using artificial light can prove challenging due to the short working distances involved. The camera's built-in, pop-up unit is designed to cover subjects 5-15ft away and, as your subject will be much closer than this, your camera's integral flash won't be useful. Also, the high fixed position of a hotshoe-mounted speedlight means that the flash burst may miss or only partly illuminate close subjects. However, flashgun units provide far greater flexibility, having the ability to be used off-camera. Positioning the flash off-camera allows greater control over the light's direction. Off-axis lighting will create contrast as tiny shadows are formed on the subject's

surface, enhancing texture and aiding sharpness. If using a tripod, it is often possible to handhold the flash in position while releasing the shutter using the other. You can position and angle the flash how you want, then review results to see if you need to move the flash closer or further away. You may also discover that you need more (or less) diffusion.

While this type of off-camera flash set-up is well-suited to static subjects when the camera can also be fixed on a tripod, it isn't practical if you want to shoot handheld – if stalking insects, for example. In instances like this, a ring or macro flash is the best option, being designed specifically to illuminate close-up subjects. Unlike a conventional flashgun, a ring/macro flash is circular, attaching directly to the front of the lens via an adaptor. This design enables the flash to effectively illuminate nearby subjects from all directions at once, providing even, shadowless light. While this might sound ideal for close-ups, in practice the resulting light can look unnaturally flat. To overcome this, most modern ring/macro flash units boast more than one flash tube, which can be controlled independently. This allows photographers to vary the output ratio between them in order to create shadows and more natural,

They're expensive, but the ultimate in macro flash units have two (or more) heads that can be angled and rotated into any position for natural lighting.

three-dimensional looking results. You can also buy ringflash adaptors which convert ordinary flashguns into a makeshift ringflash by redirecting the flash burst to a circular unit which fits around the lens. Another option is LED ringlights, which can be found for under £30 – see our test on page 140.

Whatever subject you are shooting, don't be afraid to use artificial light if it will benefit your shots. However, your goal should be to create results that look as natural and authentic as possible.

THOMAS SHAHAN

Depth-of-field

While normally depth-of-field – the zone of acceptable sharpness – falls one-third in front of the point of focus and two-thirds beyond it, when shooting close-ups, this ratio changes. At higher magnifications, it falls more evenly, with depth-of-field being spread fairly equally either side of the point of focus. It is inherently shallow, though, with depth-of-field growing progressively more limited as the level of magnification increases. While working with such a shallow depth-of-field can prove challenging, it can also benefit your images. Foreground and background detail is quickly thrown out of focus, helping your subject stand out against its surroundings. To do this, opt for a large magnification with a wide aperture around f/2.8 to f/5.6. This is also ideal for handheld shooting as the shutter speed will be faster, therefore freezing motion.

When depth-of-field is shallow, parts of your subject will inevitably begin to drift out of focus. To some degree this is acceptable, but to help make the most of the available depth-of-field, keep your camera's sensor plane parallel to the subject. This is because there is only one geometrical plane of complete sharpness, so you want to keep as much of the subject as possible within this zone (main picture). For a more abstract look, do the opposite, intentionally aligning the plane of sharpest focus so that it is perpendicular to your subject to highlight very specific areas or detail (inset, below right). When you want your subject to be rendered sharply, you need to extend depth-of-field with a narrower aperture – for example, f/11 or f/16 (inset, below left). At high levels of magnification, this still won't generate a particularly large depth-of-field, so you will still need to focus with care. A large zone of sharpness is useful when shooting still-life subjects and documentary-style images of plant-life. However, you should avoid selecting your lens's smallest aperture as image quality softens due to diffraction. Shutter speed is also lengthened, so a tripod will be essential to avoid shake. Generally, large apertures are most suited to static subjects, studio work or when using flash.

Focal length: 90mm · Exposure: F/2.8, 1/250 sec · ISO 100

SP 90mm
F/2.8 Di VC USD MACRO 1:1

Refined for higher detail and sharper
Macro and Portrait photographs.

**New 90mm Macro lens delivers superior image quality –
incorporating state-of-the-art optical technology and
image stabilization.**

Tamron's classic 90mm Macro lens is reborn to let you shoot exquisite
images of outstanding sharpness. Compatible with full-size SLR
cameras, this new, high-resolution lens lets the photographer capture
the moment's atmosphere.

TAMRON
NEW
Di Series

 **5 YEAR WARRANTY**   www.facebook.com/TamronUK

Compatible mounts: Canon, Nikon, Sony*
Model F004   Di (Digitally Integrated) lens designed for digital APS-C and full-size SLR cameras, with lens hood. Compatible mounts: Canon, Nikon, Sony*
* The Sony mount does not include VC, as Sony digital SLR bodies include image stabilization functionality. The Sony lens is designated as "SP 90mm F/2.8 Di MACRO 1:1 USD".

www.tamron.co.uk

TAMRON
New eyes for industry

Intro 2020 Ltd. Priors Way, Maidenhead, Berkshire SL6 2HP Tel: 01628 674411

Which exposure mode for macro photography?

There are many functions you need to master, none more important than your choice of exposure mode

CLOSE-UP PHOTOGRAPHY presents many challenges, so it's important that you have your camera set up correctly so that when presented with the ideal scenario for great images, you're set up and ready to capture perfect results. With digital cameras boasting an incredible range of functions, it's easy to lose track of some of the settings, so it's important that before you start taking pictures, you ensure the camera's key features, such as AF, metering and White Balance, are set up correctly. Doing so means that when you are ready to begin capturing stunning images, your camera is too.

Top of the list of functions you need to set correctly is the exposure modes. The basic job of an exposure mode is to ensure that just the right amount of light reaches the image sensor to record a 'correctly' exposed image, using a suitable aperture and shutter speed combination. Most cameras offer the core four exposure modes – program, aperture-priority, shutter-priority and manual – plus a range of specialist program modes biased to specific subjects, such as sport, landscape, portraits and close-ups.

All the modes are designed to give the correct exposure, but where they differ is in how they influence the final result, the amount of control you have over the aperture and shutter speed selected, and also how quick and easy they are to use. With macro photography, as the relationship between apertures and depth-of-field is so important, you must choose a mode that allows you to determine the aperture being used. In most instances, your best bet is to use aperture-priority, as you choose the aperture setting leaving the camera to set the appropriate shutter speed.

More experienced photographers may want to try manual mode, which allows full control of apertures and shutter speeds. This is particularly useful in tricky lighting situations such as backlighting, as changes to exposure can be made quickly. For most situations though, using aperture-priority mode is best.

An introduction to apertures

They're an important part of picture-taking and essential to understand if you want to take good shots, so let's get to grips with apertures

THE MOST IMPORTANT technical aspect of photography is creating a well-exposed image. Okay, focusing is important, too – there's no point producing perfectly exposed shots if they're out of focus – though autofocus systems can take care of that for you. The same can be said of exposure, too, to an extent. You can set your DSLR to program or full-auto mode and, more often than not, it'll get the exposure spot-on without you having to think about the settings being used. However, the two main controls that make that exposure happen – the lens aperture and the shutter speed – also perform other important tasks that have a big influence on the success of every photo you take, so understanding what they do and how they do it is crucial.

The main role of the lens aperture is to control the flow of light through the lens, which it does using a series of f/numbers (see below). But there's more, because those f/numbers also control how much of the scene or subject you're shooting will record in focus.

This 'zone' of sharp focus is commonly referred to as depth-of-field. The wider the aperture is (the lower the f/number), the less depth-of-field you get, and the smaller the aperture (the higher the f/number), the more depth-of-field you get. So, if you're shooting portraits, for example, you're more likely to use a wide aperture to reduce depth-of-field and throw the background out of focus, while for landscapes, it's common to use a smaller aperture to give increased depth-of-field, so everything is recorded in focus.

We'll cover these areas in more detail later, but suffice to say that because depth-of-field varies so much across the aperture range, knowing which aperture is set and the effect it's likely to have on the final image is crucial, and that task is down to you.

Do you dabble with electronic flash? Then aperture choice again takes priority because it also controls the flash exposure. The reason is that the duration of a burst of flash is so brief that the camera's shutter speed becomes irrelevant – providing it's not faster than the flash sync speed of the camera. Achieving an accurate exposure is based solely on how much of that flash burst is allowed to enter the lens, which in turn is dictated by the size of the lens aperture – if the aperture is too big you'll get overexposure; too small and the image will be underexposed.

Aperture basics

The aperture, which is an iris formed by a series of blades in your lens, closes down to form a hole through which light passes. The hole size is governed by a series of f/numbers, something like this: f/1.4, f/2, f/2.8, f/4, f/5.6, f/8, f/11, f/16, f/22, f/32 (shown below).

As the f/number gets bigger, the aperture itself gets smaller, and vice versa. More precisely, each aperture in the sequence admits half as much light as the previous one moving down the scale from left to right, and twice as much as the previous one moving right to left. The range of f/numbers offered by a lens varies – a 50mm prime lens may go from f/1.4 to f/16, whereas a 70-200mm telezoom may have a range from f/4 to f/32. It's the maximum (lowest) and minimum (highest) f/numbers that differ from lens to lens, but the core range can be found in all modern lenses.

As the aperture is set electronically in DSLRs, there are also intermediate f/numbers between the main f/stops, usually in third-of-a-stop increments: between f/4 and f/5.6, for example, you can set f/4.5 and f/5; between f/5.6 and f/8, there's f/6.3 and f/7.1; and so on. This gives you more precise control over the exposure.

The way you set the aperture depends on the exposure mode your DSLR is set to. Of all the exposure modes on offer, aperture-priority is generally most useful. This is where you control the aperture; if light levels fluctuate – which means the exposure has to be adjusted – the camera does that by changing the shutter speed. The same applies if you dial in exposure compensation. In shutter-priority, the opposite happens; the shutter speed remains fixed and the camera changes the aperture, which is not what you want for depth-of-field control. Manual mode works well, too, because both the aperture and

Above: Wide aperture
A larger aperture (ie lower f/number) results in a shot with a shallow depth-of-field, meaning the surrounding area falls softly out of focus.

Above right: Small aperture
A smaller aperture (ie higher f/number) results in a shot with sharper details. The smaller the aperture, the more front-to-back sharpness you're likely to achieve.

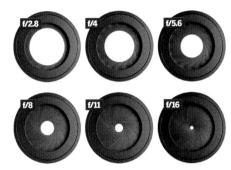

shutter speed remain fixed until you physically change them, but it's a slower mode to use and it's easier to mess up the exposure in changing light.

Exposure modes

Av **Aperture-priority (A or Av):** As the name implies, it's intended to give you full control over the aperture that is set – you change the f/number by turning a dial until the one you want is displayed. The shutter speed automatically changes to match the aperture so that correct exposure is maintained.

Tv **Shutter-priority (S or Tv):** If you're shooting in shutter-priority mode then you select the shutter speed you want and the camera matches it with the aperture required to achieve correct exposure. All you do, therefore, is adjust the shutter speed until the camera sets the aperture you want.

P **Program mode (P):** The camera sets the aperture and shutter speed automatically, but you can shift the combination using the input dial until the aperture you want is displayed.

M **Manual mode (M):** You set both the shutter speed and aperture, so select the aperture you want then adjust the shutter speed until correct exposure is indicated.

ROSS HODDINOTT

Take care with f/stops

With static subjects like fungi, shoot at different apertures and select your favourite setting.

ROSS HODDINOTT

Apertures FAQs

Q What's the connection between aperture and lens speed?

A Lens speed refers to the maximum (widest) aperture a lens has. For example, some 70-200mm telezooms have a maximum aperture of f/2.8, while others only go as wide as f/4. Where a lens in any category has a wider maximum aperture than most, it's said to be a 'fast' lens; so a 70-200mm f/2.8 would be classed as fast, as would a 16-35mm f/2.8 or an 85mm f/1.4, whereas a 75-300mm f/4-5.6 zoom would be considered 'slow'. Fast lenses are more expensive and usually bigger/heavier than their slower stablemates because their optical design is more complicated and needs more glass.

Q What's the benefit of a fast lens over a slower one?

A The immediate benefit is that by being able to set a wider maximum aperture, you can use a faster shutter speed – that's why sports and wildlife photographers favour them. You might be limited to 1/125sec with a lens wide open at f/4, but in the same situation with a lens that has a maximum aperture of f/2.8, you could shoot at 1/250sec. That's because going one stop wider lets twice as much light through and the shutter only needs to be open for half as long. Another benefit, especially with telephoto and telezoom lenses, is that you can achieve a shallower depth-of-field with a wider maximum aperture to isolate your subject and throw the background out of focus. You also get a brighter viewfinder image aiding composition and focusing, especially in low light.

Q Are f/numbers the same from lens to lens - for instance, is f/8 on a 70-200mm zoom the same as f/8 on a 17-40mm zoom?

A Yes, all f/numbers admit the same amount of light, regardless of the lens focal length, so if you switch from one lens to another in any situation, the shutter speed you need to achieve correct exposure is the same if the aperture on each lens is the same.

Q Why does the maximum aperture on some zooms vary, such as with a 75-300mm f/4-5.6?

A Zoom lenses use a number of glass elements in various groups or clusters to achieve a variable focal length. As you zoom through the focal length range from the wider end to the longer end, those elements move to magnify the subject. In less expensive zooms, the optical design is such that the effective maximum aperture becomes smaller as focal length increases in order to keep the cost of the lens down. Zooms that have a constant maximum aperture through the focal length range are more costly because they incorporate a more complicated optical design.

Q Why is it that if I take a photograph that suffers from flare, the flare spots are often a similar shape to the lens aperture?

A Because flare is caused by non-image forming light bouncing around inside the lens, sometimes some of it reflects off the diaphragm that forms the aperture, hence why you get aperture-shaped flare! It can look effective on some shots, but is generally best avoided by using a lens hood or shading the front of the lens so it's protected from stray light.

Depth-of-field preview

Assessing depth-of-field – how much of a scene will be recorded in focus – is tricky with DSLRs. That's because the aperture in lenses is set to its lowest f/number (widest aperture) until you press the shutter; so the depth-of-field you see in the viewfinder is what you'd get if you took the shot with the lens wide open. To get an idea of the depth-of-field you'll achieve at the aperture you're going to use for the shot, you can use your DSLR's depth-of-field preview – there's usually a button on the front of the camera. Press it to manually stop the aperture down to the f/number set. If you select a small aperture, the viewfinder will go dark when you depress the preview button, because you're letting much less light in through a smaller hole. Initially you'll find it difficult to see much at all, but if you keep your eye to the viewfinder, it will adjust to the lower light levels and you'll begin to see the image more clearly – enough to establish what's in focus. If you're a Canon user, you have the advantage of assessing depth-of-field using LiveView on the bright LCD monitor.

Apertures and close-ups

Your point of focus can make a good close-up shot brilliant. Here are the pros' secrets to achieving amazing macro results…

AS YOU'VE ALREADY discovered, the wider the aperture (low f/number), the narrower depth-of-field becomes. However, this effect is exaggerated further when shooting close-ups, as it also grows progressively shallower at higher magnifications. The zone of sharpness can be wafer-thin at reproduction ratios in the region of 1:1 (life-size), so in order to capture pin-sharp close-ups using wide apertures, your focusing and technique must be good.

With depth-of-field being so limited at wider apertures, you might assume that a smaller f/number would be better to generate a larger zone of sharpness. Doing so, though, can sometimes bring distracting foreground and background detail into focus, creating messy backdrops that draw the eye away from your subject. Selecting a higher f/number will also result in a much slower corresponding shutter speed, which can be impractical when working handheld or if photographing moving subjects, like insects or flowers that are windblown.

Practical considerations aside, there are also many aesthetic advantages to employing a wide aperture when shooting close-ups. It will help you throw the subject's surroundings beautifully out of focus, creating a diffused wash of colour that will help your subject stand out boldly – a technique we mentioned earlier, known as differential focusing. For example, when photographing insects or wild flowers, an aperture in the region of f/4 or f/5.6 will ensure only the subject itself is sharp and that the background is clutter-free without the need to 'garden' surrounding vegetation or alter viewpoint. In order to maximise the available depth-of-field at any given aperture, try to keep your camera's sensor plane parallel to the subject. This is because there is only one geometrical plane of complete sharpness,

so you want to place as much of your subject within this plane as possible.

Whether you're photographing wildlife, plant life or still-lifes, selecting a large aperture can prove a highly useful creative tool when using a macro lens or close-up attachment, emphasising your point of focus. Virtually everything in front of and behind your point of focus will drift progressively out of focus, offering all kinds of creative potential. For example, you may want to place your point of focus on a flower's petals or stamens while allowing the rest of the flower to drift attractively out of focus. The trick is to achieve just enough depth-of-field to ensure your background subject is nicely diffused but remains recognisable. If your camera has a preview button, use it to view the effect. Adjust the f/number if more or less depth-of-field is required. This type of selective focusing can create striking, artistic results and convey far more about the subject's size, beauty and design than had it been sharp all over.

A wide aperture allows close-up photographers to be far more creative with focusing, but it's not all good news. The shallow depth-of-field created by using a low f/number means focusing has to be pinpoint accurate. With the zone of sharpness potentially just a matter of millimetres, achieving sharp results handheld isn't easy. Whenever possible, use a tripod. This will allow you to place your point of focus with far greater accuracy. In situations where using a tripod isn't practical, take a larger sequence of shots to ensure at least one is correctly focused. Manual focus is best as autofocus can struggle to lock on to close-up subjects. Better still, use your camera's LiveView and zoom into the area of interest before carefully fine-tuning your focus accordingly.

Pro tip: Ross Hoddinott

"When shooting close-ups, depth-of-field is often very shallow due to the high level of magnification. As a result, the general perception is that a high f/number should be used. I disagree, though; I rarely employ high f/numbers when shooting wild flowers and insects. First, that would result in a slower shutter speed, which is often undesirable when shooting wildlife in natural light. Second, doing so can bring too much distracting background detail into focus, creating messy backdrops. I often use wider apertures in the region of f/2.8 to f/8. Such a narrow depth-of-field helps my subject stand out boldly against its backdrop. Results can look striking, but focusing does have to be pinpoint accurate. To ensure you keep the subject acceptably sharp throughout, position your camera parallel to the subject to maximise depth-of-field. Also, if possible, focus manually using LiveView to allow you to zoom in and place your point of focus precisely. A shallow depth-of-field can certainly prove a powerful aesthetic tool for close-ups."

Altering depth-of-field

Anyone can capture a sharp image, it is where you put the blur that really matters! This picture sequence of a banded demoiselle was taken using the same viewpoint and point of focus – only the level of depth-of-field has been altered.

The sequence here shows how background detail becomes more noticeable and distracting in the images taken using a smaller aperture. A wide aperture will help you isolate your subject, emphasising its shape and form, but position your point of focus with great care.

f/2.8

f/5.6

f/11

f/16

f/22

Close encounter!
Where you position your point of
focus can have a dramatic effect
on the impact of your images.

Fundamentals of lighting

Turn your average garden flora photography into beautiful still-lifes by learning how to master and manipulate the basics of daylight

JUST LIKE ANY other subject, lighting is the key ingredient to success when photographing the plants growing and flowering in your garden. Good lighting will make your images stand out from the crowd, while poor lighting will undermine your efforts. Early morning and late evening light are traditionally the best times for photography, with the sun's low position providing warmth and softness to the quality of light. However, neighbouring buildings, hedges and fencing mean that many gardens fall into deep shade prematurely. As a consequence, photographers may be forced to take pictures during the day instead. Daytime light can prove harsh and contrasty. However, when shooting close-ups, photographers possess far more control over lighting. It is possible to manipulate light, using shade, altering shooting position or through the use of flash or a reflector.

Bright, overcast lighting is an underrated form of illumination, but one that is well-suited to plant photography. Subtle, overcast light reduces the glare from foliage, restoring natural colour saturation. It also reduces contrast, allowing photographers to record fine detail that might otherwise appear washed out in direct light. In fact, if the light is particularly harsh, casting your subject into shade – using your own shadow, or even an umbrella – is a useful trick for reducing contrast and producing a

better result. Shooting in overcast light isn't without drawbacks, though. It is important to note that shutter speeds are longer as a result, so if it is windy there is an increased risk of unintentional subject blur. It is also trickier to focus and compose your shot with any accuracy in windy weather. Thankfully, when shooting in a garden environment, it is usually possible to find a sheltered corner where you will be unaffected by blustery conditions.

On-camera flash and frontal lighting can create flat, shadowless light, which is often best avoided. Overhead light from the midday sun can cast dark, ugly shadows beneath the subject, which can be a problem if shooting from a low or parallel viewpoint. In this type of light, a small handheld silver/white reflector is essential. By holding the reflector adjacent and angling it so that light is bounced back onto the subject to relieve dark shadows, it is possible to balance the light and create a more attractively lit close-up. Alter the light's intensity by moving the reflector closer or further away.

Side-lighting is well-suited to garden subjects, enhancing texture and creating a greater impression of depth in a photo. For more dramatic results, opt for backlighting. Backlighting will highlight fine detail, like hairy foliage, stamens and veining. This type of light works well with translucent subjects like leaves.

Shooting backlit plants

ALL IMAGES ROSS HODDINOTT

When shooting garden plants, backlighting is a very creative form of illumination. It highlights shape, form and miniature detail that might otherwise get overlooked. It is particularly well-suited to translucent subjects – for example, backlighting will emphasise every tiny vein found running through a leaf. However, this form of lighting is also one of the most technically challenging. When shooting toward the light source, the risk of flare is enhanced. Therefore, attach a lens hood or carefully shield the front of the lens using your hand or a piece of card. Also, backlit subjects are more likely to fool a digital SLR's multi-zone meter. Metering can be erratic at times, so it is important to regularly assess exposure when shooting backlit subjects. Review your histogram screen and be prepared to adjust your exposure compensation settings.

Garden lighting tutorial

To explain the basics of using light in a garden photography situation, nature photographer Ross Hoddinott ventures into his back garden armed with his DSLR. His task is to shoot a flower while contending with bright sunshine, using just a tripod and a reflector. A collapsible silver/white reflector can be picked up for as little as £15 to £20, while a decent tripod (essential for garden photography) will set you back around £80 to £100.

Set-up

1 Try a large aperture In deciding to shoot a handful of close-ups, I opt for a parallel viewpoint and select a wide aperture of f/2.8 to create a shallow depth-of-field. However, the bright, overhead sun is creating a dark, ugly shadow beneath the flower and along its stem.

2 Use a reflector When working in close proximity to the subject, a burst of camera flash can look artificial unless carefully regulated, so a reflector is often a better option. I simply hold it in place nearby and angle the reflected light onto the flower to relieve the shadow areas.

3 Shoot in shade You can reduce contrast by taking photographs in shade. If there are no passing clouds that will oblige, simply use your own shadow to cast over smaller garden subjects. Shooting in shade can lead to longer exposure times, so be wary of blur in your shots.

4 Increase ISO I increase the ISO sensitivity of my DSLR from 100 to 200 to get a faster shutter speed. I then wait for a lull in the gentle breeze before releasing the shutter. This time the shot is pin-sharp. By controlling the light, this image looks much better than the original.

Backlit subjects
Adding backlight to subjects like leaves can highlight detail that would otherwise have been invisible.

Exposing for close-ups

Using your body and a reflector can help you expose correctly when shooting outdoor close-ups. This quick tutorial talks you through it

Ross Hoddinott: While textures, abstract details, still-lifes, nature and flora are all good close-up subjects, remember that shooting at high levels of magnification can be a challenge – that's because depth-of-field grows progressively shallower and any subject or camera movement appears greatly enhanced. It is not all bad news, though. Due to the small size of the subject and the close proximity from which you are working, close-up photographers have far greater control over the lighting and exposure of their shots.

Many close-up images fail simply due to the quality of the light. Pictures taken outdoors in harsh, direct light (during the midday sun, for example) can prove uneven and contrasty – resulting in either bright highlights or areas of dark shade. Not only can the results look disappointing, but this type of light can cause exposure problems, as a DSLR's metering system can be easily deceived when the subject is a contrasting mixture of light and dark.

To create a more even exposure, shadows should be relieved. A burst of artificial light is one option, but flash can appear quite harsh and unnatural. Also, a hotshoe-mounted flash – or a DSLR's built-in unit – may well miss, or only partially illuminate, a close-up subject due to the short camera-to-subject working distance. Most close-up photographers prefer to use natural light when possible. The best way to do this is using a handheld reflector to bounce the sunlight back into the shadowy areas.

If the light is really strong and intense, close-up photographers should consider shading their subject. This might sound like an odd thing to do, but overcast light can prove more flattering for a number of subjects, particularly flowers and foliage. The reduction in contrast allows photographers to capture fine, intricate detail and better colour saturation. Shading your subject – using your body or placing your camera bag nearby to block the light – can work well in combination with a little bounced light from a reflector. Together, they can help you to create subtly lit, perfectly exposed close-ups. Our step-by-step guide below shows you how.

Watch out for shake!

Intentionally shading your subject to help balance exposure lengthens the exposure time. This can increase the risk of shake, so be sure to switch on the image-stabiliser or use a sturdy tripod

Reflectors

Reflectors are usually collapsible discs of material. They are available in a variety of sizes. The larger they are, the greater the area of reflected light – a 30cm or 60cm reflector is normally quite sufficient to illuminate miniature subjects. Reflectors are typically white on one side, for neutral-looking results, and silver or gold on the other, allowing photographers to alter the quality or warmth of the reflected light. The reflector should be positioned to direct light onto the area you require, adding extra light to your subject and relieving harsh shadows. Moving the reflector closer or further away will alter the light's intensity, allowing close-up photographers to easily manipulate the natural light and to regulate the effect by sight. They are inexpensive to buy, but you can make your own by attaching tin foil to a piece of card.

1 Compose your shot Some attractive, bright yellow flowers catch my eye during a visit to a local public garden. I want to capture a frame-filling image, so attach a macro lens to my Nikon D700. I keep the flower head still by holding it with a Plamp, fixed to a tripod leg. I compose my image and rely on the D700's matrix metering. However, with the flower being partly in shade, the result is very contrasty and the highlights on the petals appear bright and distracting.

2 Use a reflector To relieve dark shadow areas, I bounce light onto the flower using a small reflector. This balances the light, reducing the level of contrast. I hold the reflector opposite the flower and carefully direct the light until I achieve the level of illumination I require. The result is better, and the dark shadows are greatly alleviated, but the light is still uneven and the shadows cast by surrounding foliage distracting. I decide to change my viewpoint.

Final image

Final image
I move the reflector slighter further away and direct the bounced light with more care, which gives a more natural-looking result. Though this approach wouldn't be practical if shooting timid wildlife, such as insects or reptiles, in this instance it has really brought this floral image alive. Using a combination of shade and reflected light has given me far more control over lighting and allowed me to create a perfect exposure. I'm really happy with this shot.

3 Shoot in shadow When shooting close-ups of small subjects, you can manipulate the light easily. To create a more balanced exposure and eliminate distracting highlights – caused by the sunlight reflecting on the petals – I cast my shadow over the flower, releasing the shutter using a remote. While this results in a longer exposure time, overcast light is ideal for many close-up subjects, especially flowers. However, the result looks a little dull and lifeless.

4 Reflect light Shading the flower worked well, but I want to add more life to my shot by adding some reflected light. Again, I position my reflector nearby to bounce light on to the plant. On this occasion, I hold the reflector too near and the light is too intense. The light looks flat and artificial – as if a burst of flash has been used, proving that reflected light needs to be applied with care. I'm still not happy with the viewpoint so decide to change it a little again.

Spot-metering for small subjects

Ross Hoddinott explains how spot-metering makes capturing smaller subjects easier

NO TTL METERING system is foolproof – they probably never will be. Even the most sophisticated multi-zone metering patterns are not immune to error. Subjects against very light or dark backgrounds are renowned for causing problems, particularly small subjects like my speciality – insects. This is because multi-zone metering is designed to divide the scene into numerous zones. The camera takes individual readings from each zone, then examines the various readings before calculating an average. Usually, this is an effective way of achieving correct exposure, but very dark or light backgrounds can prove deceptive. A dark backdrop can fool the camera into thinking the subject is darker than it actually is. Therefore, it selects a longer exposure than is needed, resulting in the subject being overexposed. In contrast, a very light background will make the camera believe the subject is brighter than reality, and consequently set a shorter exposure. This results in the main subject being too dark or underexposed. While you can remedy this by applying a little exposure compensation, a more accurate method is to switch from your camera's multi-zone metering system to spot-metering.

Spot-metering is the most precise form of TTL metering. It calculates exposure from a small percentage of the image frame, without being influenced by the brightness in other areas. Typically, the spot meter employs a reading from a central circle covering around 3% of the frame. While spot-metering offers photographers more control over the accuracy of exposure, it is also the technique which relies most on the user's input. It requires you to point the metering sensor directly at the area you wish to meter from. The DSLR then calculates exposure based purely on this. Using spot-metering makes it possible to achieve precise readings for small subjects within the frame. Spot-metering is often best used together with manual exposure mode. Point the spot-metering area at the subject you wish to meter from, such as a mid-tone or grey card, and then, using the command dial, align the indicator with the (0) on the +/- scale in the viewfinder. You have now set the exposure your camera recommends for the area you've manually metered. When shooting in M, this exposure value won't alter unless you adjust settings. In contrast, if you spot-meter when using an auto or semi-automatic exposure mode, you will need to employ Autoexposure Lock (AE-L) to retain your new settings. Fail to do so and your spot-meter reading will change if you adjust composition.

Step-by-step to spot-metering for a small subjects

Insects and flora look striking contrasted against a light or dark backdrop. However, this type of situation can prove to be an exposure headache. While I normally rely on my DSLR's multi-zone metering, I know it can be fooled by a predominantly dark or light backdrop. So I often switch to spot-metering mode to allow me to take more accurate readings. Rather than fiddle about locking exposure setting using the AE-L button, I keep the camera in manual mode, take a spot-meter reading from an area on the subject which I believe to be mid-tone. Once I set the camera's recommended settings, I know they won't alter unless I decide to change them. They are locked in, allowing me to concentrate on composition and focus.

Dark backgrounds

Dark backgrounds are just as likely to fool multi-zone metering, evaluating the whole scene and being fooled into thinking the subject is darker than it is. The camera will likely select a longer exposure time than is required, exposing the sensor for too long and producing a result that is overexposed with washed-out colours. Again, the best way to overcome this problem is to switch to spot-metering mode and take a more accurate reading from a part of the subject you consider to be mid-tone. This is a fast, precise way to obtain the right exposure. It is also a good method to use to achieve the correct exposure when photographing backlit subjects.

1 Dial in settings I notice this dragonfly resting on a reed near the water's edge. It looks striking against the brightly lit water. With my camera in manual, I select an aperture of f/8 and then slowly move into position. Using multi-zone metering and the exposure scale in the viewfinder, my camera recommends a shutter speed of 1/500sec. However, the result is underexposed.

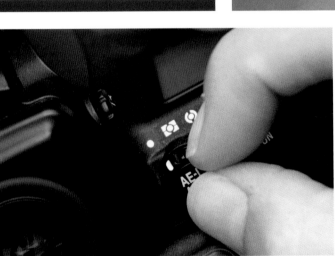

2 Switch to spot meter The bright background has clearly fooled my camera's metering so I switch the camera to spot-metering mode instead. This will allow me to meter from a small area of the subject and achieve a more accurate, reliable setting. On my camera, the lever is on the body itself and quick to select. Check your manual to learn how to switch to spot-metering mode.

Final image
Using spot-metering in manual has taken the hassle out of capturing this little critter. Job done!

3 Adjust shutter speed I direct the spot-metering circle at the dragonfly's dark, hairy back. Keeping aperture at f/8, I alter the shutter speed to 1/125sec – the suggested exposure length for my spot-meter reading. However, I've made a mistake. By metering from such a dark area of the insect's body, the camera is fooled into overexposure and the resulting image is too light.

4 Check histogram A quick glance at the image's histogram reveals my mistake, with a sharp peak at the right of the graph. I quickly remedy the problem by aiming the spot sensor at the dragonfly's blue abdomen – a good mid-tone that should provide a more accurate reading. I adjust shutter speed accordingly to 1/250sec. The result is a correct and balanced exposure.

Backgrounds and depth-of-field

Give your images more impact by mastering the relationship between apertures and depth-of-field to isolate your subjects

A MESSY, CLUTTERED background will often undermine otherwise good images. Even if composition, lighting and exposure are spot-on, distracting foreground and background detail will weaken the overall photo. Pause for a moment to let your eye wander around the frame. Anything that doesn't complement your subject should be excluded – grasses, dead leaves, twigs or bright highlights. Do this by 'gardening' to remove certain aspects from the frame using scissors (carefully and sensitively, of course!) or by changing your shooting position to alter depth-of-field.

Depth-of-field is one of the most important creative elements of close-up photography. The relative lack of distance between the subject and the camera's sensor means the area that appears sharp will be very limited – depending

on how you set your shot up, it could be mere millimetres, even when using a small aperture! Therefore, macro photography requires pinpoint focusing. A good knowledge of apertures is the most important single factor, as the f/number you choose will have the greatest influence on the amount of depth-of-field in your image.

One notable difference between macro and other types of photography is how depth-of-field is evenly distributed in front of and behind the point of focus. In other words, the amount of the scene that appears to be sharp will be equal both in front of and behind the point of focus, about 50:50. In normal range photography, it's more often 30:70, with increasingly more in focus behind the subject at greater distances.

It is important to have an idea of how much depth-of-field suits your subject. For abstract close-ups, such as on a flower, shallow depth-of-field is best, keeping only a small part in focus. See the panel below to see how to do it.

The position of your DSLR's sensor is also crucial. To keep your subject sharp, your subject must be square-on to the camera. By rotating or tilting the camera, you can reduce depth-of-field further as the subject will move out of the focused area and become softer in the distance.

✓ Camera shake

The smaller the aperture (higher f/number), the more depth-of-field, which means less light reaches the sensor. To maximise front-to-back sharpness, you may also get a slower shutter speed, so make sure you use a tripod

Assessing depth-of-field

There are two ways to check depth-of-field in-camera without actually taking a shot. The traditional depth-of-field preview button, found on most mid-range and high-end DSLRs (and some entry-level models) near the lens mount or shutter-release button, can be used to close the lens iris to the selected aperture, providing a dark viewfinder image that reveals the depth-of-field in the scene. If you're a Canon EOS user and your camera has a LiveView facility (all recent models have LiveView), then you can check out depth-of-field in a similar fashion using the LCD monitor.

Get focused!

Depth-of-field is controlled via the lens aperture; wide settings (for example, f/2.8 or f/4) produce a shallow depth-of-field, while small apertures (f/16 or f/22) help achieve back-to-front sharpness.

The f/number you select will help dictate the look, feel and mood of the end result, so experiment. Although focusing has to be pinpoint accurate, a shallow depth-of-field is a useful creative tool. It allows you to isolate your subject against an attractive wash of colour and direct the viewer's eye to an intended focal point – a flower's stamens or a single petal, for example. Doing this can create very arty, abstract results as seen here.

'Declutter' your subject

To create a flattering, clean and diffused background, a small aperture of f/4 was selected. A handful of grasses were removed from the flower's background to keep it free of distraction. The result is an attractive flower portrait. The shot proves that it is worthwhile taking a few extra moments to consider the subject's background before finally releasing the shutter.

Close-up composition

Composition is just as important in macro work as it is in landscapes or still-lifes. Find out the secrets here

Ross Hoddinott: Composition is the skill of arranging the key elements within the viewfinder so that they are visually pleasing. In reality, the difference between a poorly or well-composed image is often subtle, but if you get the composition wrong, the image's impact can be greatly reduced. With experience, your compositional skills should grow more natural and intuitive, but beginners often need to make a more conscious effort in order to get things right.

Whatever the subject matter, good composition is vital, but it could be argued that it is rarely more important than when shooting close-ups. The level of magnification highlights any imperfections – including those of composition – so precise framing is essential. All the general 'rules' of composition can be applied to close-up photography, but of these, the rule-of-thirds remains the most relevant. Simply imagining the image space divided into nine equal parts by two horizontal and two vertical lines can usually make a big difference if you try to place key subject matter along these lines, or their intersections.

Depth-of-field may not extend beyond more than a few millimetres when shooting at a high reproduction ratio, making the use of 'lead-in lines' less common in close-up photography. The limited depth-of-field synonymous with close-up photography is not always disadvantageous – it can prove to be a useful compositional and creative tool. When shooting close-ups, you can render practically everything, other than your key subject, in soft focus. Doing so can direct the viewer's eye to an intended focal point. You can isolate your subject from its surroundings, creating strong compositions. The best effect will often be achieved using a relatively large aperture of f/4 or even f/2.8. However, when employing such a narrow depth-of-field, focusing needs to be accurate, so the use of a tripod will prove helpful.

Set up Some digital SLRs allow you to overlay a grid in the viewfinder to assist the user with composition. This custom setting is normally selected via one of the camera's set-up menus. Refer to your user manual for more information on accessing this function.

1 Fill the frame Whatever the subject, thoughtful composition is essential. After noticing this dragonfly, I attach a 105mm macro lens and opt for an overhead viewpoint. I fill the viewfinder with the insect, but it looks rather boring and static with the insect central in the frame.

2 Use rule-of-thirds I adjust my composition so that the dragonfly is now off-centre to the left. I move a little further away to create more space around the subject. The result looks better, but the image is still static with the dragonfly's body composed parallel to the edge of the frame.

3 Use angles Keeping the dragonfly positioned centre-left, I angle the camera slightly so that the dragonfly's body isn't so parallel. The composition still isn't right, though. The empty space is adding little to the shot, as the dragonfly is angled away from it. Instead, the insect appears to be looking directly out of the frame and, consequently, the viewer's eye follows its gaze out of shot.

4 Aim towards negative space By altering composition subtly, the image is transformed. By placing the dragonfly to the right – on a dividing third – so that it is pointing into the open space, the composition looks far stronger. The image is more balanced and the empty space, intentionally left around the insect, adds to the image's aesthetic appeal.

Final image
Using the tips from our steps
shows how spending a bit of
time on your composition can
make a world of difference to
your finished image.

Try cropping your close-ups

Dynamic images often come from doing things out of the ordinary – while filling the frame with your subject can work, cropping can also result in great images

Ross Hoddinott: When applied to your close-up photography, the compositional 'rules' will improve your images more often than not. However, rules are meant to be broken. They should be treated as guidelines: follow them too religiously and you risk stifling your creativity.

Composition is a subjective thing and each and every picture-taking opportunity should be treated individually. For example, placing your subject off-centre on a 'third' is not guaranteed to produce the best result. In the right situation, placing your subject centrally, big and bold in the frame can create a powerfully dynamic result.

You may also want to break the 'rules' if you wish to highlight a subject's symmetry. Large flowers – like oxeye daisies and dahlias – are among the most photogenic symmetrical subjects. Placing the flowers centrally in the viewfinder will help emphasise these symmetrical qualities. You could also consider cropping the image into a square format during post-processing to further highlight its symmetrical form. Cropping an image can vastly alter and improve composition, so don't overlook using the Crop Tool in Photoshop.

When photographing wildlife close-ups – insects, reptiles and amphibians, for instance – photographers are normally encouraged to compose the image with more space in front of the subject than behind it. This creates empty space to absorb the creature's 'gaze'. While this type of composition often works well, placing your subject closer to the edge of the frame, or towards a corner, can look even more striking – even if the subject is looking directly out of shot. Being unconventional with your composition can really grab the viewer's attention – don't be afraid to experiment.

Close-up photographers are able to manipulate a shallow depth-of-field to aid composition. Normally, you are advised to compose your main subject in the foreground, with background detail drifting pleasantly out of focus. This might normally be the most logical approach, but eye-catching results can also be achieved by placing your subject, or point of focus, further back. A wide aperture of around f/4 will ensure that the foreground is nicely blurred, leading the eye towards your intended point of focus in the background. If you wish to place your subject in context with its surroundings, select a slightly higher f/number to keep foreground detail recognisable.

Set-up

☑ Shape shifting
You can greatly alter the look and feel of an image, by simply changing the camera's orientation. A vertical composition will emphasise height while a horizontal image highlights width

1 Set up I want to create a visually striking floral close-up – a shot that will break all the rules of composition. Having bought an orange gerbera at a local florist, I place it in a vase on a table. To add impact, I cover the table with a blue cloth – creating a vibrant, contrasting backdrop. Shooting from an overhead angle, I compose the image with the flower central in the frame.

2 Zoom in and crop The previous shot looks rather uninspiring, so I decide to move closer to the flower, using the magnification of my 105mm macro lens to isolate just a section of the flower. I place the gerbera at the bottom of the frame, including only half of the flower in the shot. Normally, you are advised not to crop subjects too abruptly, but the composition still looks intentional.

3 Dissect the image Next, I try placing the flower to the far edge of the frame, so that the image space is half-flower, half-empty space. Effectively, I dissect the image in two, defying the compositional rules. The result introduces lots of impact to the image, though. In this instance, the strongest result is achieved by placing the flower to the far left of the frame, balanced with the blue background.

Final image
Using the same idea, of placing the flower in one corner of the frame, I opt for a lower viewpoint. This time, I intentionally include the flower's stem, employing a wide aperture of f/4 to throw it out of focus. Although the flower and stem are angled so that they actually lead your eye towards the top-left corner and out of the frame, the image is visually strong and eye-catching – despite breaking the rules.

4 Shoot quarters Next, I try photographing just a quarter of the flower, placing it in the corner of the frame. I take a sequence of four images: one with the flower top left; another bottom left; the third top right; and, lastly, one with the gerbera bottom right. Again, an unconventional crop strengthens the image, rather than weakens it.

5 Switch format Despite the large area of empty space, the images with the flower positioned in just one corner look dynamic and fresh. I switched the camera's orientation, as I feel a vertical composition improves the shot in this instance. Despite breaking the rules, the composition works well.

UNDERSTANDI

Macro photography gives you the chance to capture a world too small to see with the naked eye. While dedicated kit is needed, Ross Hoddinott reveals that there are cost-effective alternatives to macro lenses

HAVE A QUICK GLANCE around you. Indoors or out, we are surrounded by objects that suit being shot 'up close and personal'. Flowers, foliage, bugs, textures, machinery: the list of potential subjects goes on and on. By moving in closer, you begin to see things that you would normally ignore or overlook. Through a macro lens or close-up attachment, colour, texture and intricate detail is revealed or highlighted.

Once you've caught the 'macro bug', you'll begin seeing everyday, mundane objects in a completely different light. Suddenly, a rusty old chain or peeling paintwork presents an opportunity to capture a timeless still-life or arty abstract.

It is no surprise, then, that the popularity of close-up photography is growing by the day – and it's never been more accessible or affordable. One of the most appealing things about close-up photography is that you don't need to spend a fortune on specialist kit – a £10 set of close-up filters bought on ebay will get you started. This was exactly how my love affair with shooting all things miniature began.

By simply attaching a close-up filter, I was able to enter the realms of the miniature world around me and countless new photo opportunities followed.

Close-up photography is regarded by many as specialist and technically challenging. Limited light and wafer-thin depth-of-field are synonymous with shooting at high magnifications, but don't let this put you off. The available light can easily be supplemented by using reflectors or flash, while shallow depth-of-field can be used for creative effect.

Still not convinced? Don't take my word for it; try it for yourself. For the same cost as a new DVD or CD, you can get yourself started with some inexpensive close-up filters – hardly a big gamble. If you find close-up photography isn't for you, at worst you'll have wasted a few quid. However, more likely you will love all the new opportunities available to you to capture great, interesting images. This guide will ensure you have all the knowledge you need to get you started. So what is stopping you?

Main types of close-up kit

Macro lens page 46: A dedicated lens that is optimised for close focusing. Most offer a reproduction ratio of 1:1 (life-size).

Close-up filters page 48: These attach to the lens like any screw-in filter, but act like a magnifying glass, reducing the lens's minimum focusing distance. They are available in different strengths.

Extension tubes page 50: These are hollow tubes without optical elements that fit between camera and lens. They allow for closer focusing, thereby increasing the lens's maximum magnification. Short focal lengths give most magnification.

Reversing rings page 52: A close-up adaptor ring that allows a lens to be mounted back to front. Reversing an optic in this way creates a close-focusing lens capable of high-quality results at potentially very large magnifications.

Practical tips for better close-ups

■ **Camera shake:** Shake is a major concern. It occurs when shooting handheld with a shutter speed that is too slow to eliminate camera movement. It is common with close-ups, as the slightest movement can appear exaggerated at high magnifications. The easiest way to avoid it is to use a support like a tripod or beanbag. However, if this is not practical, set a fast shutter speed: typically, a speed of 1/125sec, or faster, will guarantee sharp images. If necessary, increase ISO to raise the shutter speed. Several macro lenses now boast image stabilisers, which allow sharp images to be produced at speeds two or three stops slower than one without.

■ **Depth-of-field:** This is the zone in front and behind the point of focus that is acceptably sharp. It is determined primarily by the lens aperture, but it is also influenced by the focal length of the lens and also the camera-to-subject distance. Close-up photography is synonymous with a very shallow depth-of-field, and at high magnification can be wafer-thin. In general photography, a small aperture of f/16 or f/22 usually gives front-to-back sharpness,

but when shooting close-ups, achieving sufficient depth-of-field can be difficult. Your focusing will need to be pin-point accurate. While working with such a shallow depth-of-field can be challenging, it can also be used creatively, allowing you to isolate the subject against an attractively diffused background, or place emphasis on their point of focus. With close-ups, the amount of depth-of-field falling in front and behind the point of focus is roughly equal.

■ **Working distance:** This is the distance between subject and lens. Close-up photographers have to work very close to their subject in order to achieve frame-filling results – particularly if using close-up filters or a reversing ring. It is an important consideration if you are photographing wildlife, as there is a greater chance of frightening the subject away if you get too close. You are also likely to block natural light from reaching the subject if positioned very close to the subject. Therefore, larger working distances are normally preferable. For this reason, longer focal length macros of 100mm or more are the best choice.

Close-up accessories

Wimberley Plamp: The Plamp works like a helping hand. It is a ball-and-socket segmented arm with clamps at either end. One end attaches to a tripod leg; the other can hold a reflector or subject in place.

Reflector: Light is often limited when shooting in close proximity to the subject. Using a small, foldaway reflector, it is possible to bounce light onto the subject. The light's intensity can be altered by moving it closer or further away.

Ringflash: A flash dedicated for close-up photography. It surrounds the lens, enabling it to illuminate close-by subjects.

NG MACRO KIT

Macro lens

A dedicated lens is the easiest (but also most expensive) option for macro photography. Here's how to choose and use one…

A MACRO IS A SPECIALIST lens optimised for close focusing, allowing it to focus far closer than a conventional lens. Thanks to its highly corrected optics, it offers high image quality and performs best at high magnifications. Macros don't require any supplementary attachments in order to achieve a – truly macro – reproduction ratio of 1:1 (life-size). This is when the subject is projected on to the imaging sensor the same size as it is in reality. The vast majority of macro lenses are produced in prime, fixed focal lengths, ranging from 40mm up to 200mm. Shorter focal lengths tend to be compact and lightweight, making them portable and easy to use handheld; while 'tele' macros provide a larger camera-to-subject distance. They are also fast: normally having a maximum aperture of f/2.8 or faster.

Such a large aperture not only helps provide a lovely bright viewfinder image – aiding pin-point focusing and composition in poor light – but the narrow depth-of-field produced at the lens's maximum aperture is ideally suited to capturing close-up images with beautifully diffused backgrounds.

A macro lens is well-suited to any close-up subject, but they are particularly popular among nature photographers, providing a more practical working distance from the subject compared to other close-up attachments. By doing so, it helps maximise the chances of success when shooting wildlife that is easily frightened away.

Being a specialist lens type, macros are generally not cheap, costing between £300 to £1,000 – depending on the brand, focal length and features. However, for the dedicated close-up enthusiast, a macro lens is a very worthwhile investment.

It is also worth noting that macros are suitable for general photography, too, being particularly popular for shooting flattering portraits and still-lifes.

The pros & cons…

✔ Razor-sharp image quality
✔ Easy to use
✔ Magnification of 1:1 (life-size)
✔ Practical working distance when using longer focal lengths
✔ Light and compact when using shorter macros
✘ Costly if you don't use regularly
✘ Longer focal lengths are heavy and need careful use for best results

Using a macro lens

The margins for error in macro photography are small, meaning that you need to concentrate more on focusing, stability and depth-of-field. Focusing is particularly important. Depth-of-field is often limited, even at small f/stops. Macro lenses are renowned for their sharpness, but at high magnifications, your subject will be recorded soft if your focusing is out by even a millimetre or two. It really can be that critical. Therefore, it is usually best to switch your macro lens to manual focus, rather than rely on AF. Doing so allows you to place the point of focus with even greater accuracy, and prevents your camera searching for focus – something AF can do when trying to focus on fine, small close-up detail. When practical, LiveView focusing can help ensure razor-sharp results, as you can magnify your desired point of focus for precise, critical focusing. The smallest camera movement looks exaggerated in close-up and it is easy to overestimate how still you can hold your camera. While using longer, heavier macros is great for providing a larger working distance, they are naturally more difficult to keep still. A tripod solves the problem, but if it is impractical to use one, select a fast shutter speed that will eliminate shake. When using short macro lenses (eg a 50mm or 70mm), you will regularly find yourself working close to the subject, meaning you often can't avoid your body or camera casting the subject in shade. Reflectors or ringflash will alleviate the problem. Depth-of-field is limited using macros, but use this to your advantage. Shallow focus can help direct the eye to your desired focal point. Remember: you don't have to record the entire subject in sharp focus. Using a macro's fast maximum aperture creates an extremely shallow focus that is perfect for capturing images where the subject, or part of it, stands out against its surroundings.

LiveView

Choosing the right macro lens

Macro lenses can be split into two categories: short and telephoto. The main advantage of short focal lengths, in the region of 50mm to 70mm, apart from being slightly cheaper, is that they are compact and lightweight, making them perfectly suited to being used handheld. They are well-suited to shooting static subjects, like flowers and still-lifes. The main drawback is that the working distance is shorter. Macros with a focal length of 70mm or more are considered to be telephoto, with lengths of 100mm, 150mm or 180mm being popular for the larger working distances they provide. On the downside, more powerful macros are longer and heavier, making it trickier to capture correctly focused, shake-free images without the aid of a support. However, if you intend shooting mostly natural history, a 'tele' macro is the best choice. Another consideration is image stabilisation. Although more costly, if your budget allows, opt for a macro with a stabiliser as it offers several stops benefit. A macro boasting internal focusing is also preferable, meaning its physical length doesn't increase when focus is adjusted.

Key features to look out for

1) Focus limiter switch: Allows you to restrict the amount of the full focus range that the autofocus system will use. This is designed to speed up autofocus and stop the lens 'hunting' for correct focus.

2) Manual focus ring: You need to be prepared to regularly use manual focus to achieve critical focus, so a wide manual focus ring with a smooth, firm action is important.

3) Tripod mount: Longer focal lengths feature a detachable tripod mount to aid stability.

Up close & personal!
For natural history images like this, the extra working distance of a 'tele' macro lens helps reduce the risk of frightening off your subject.

Macro lens best buys: A selection of some of the best macro lenses available

 £695

 £410

 £269

 £750

 £360

 £350

Canon EF 100mm f/2.8L Macro IS USM
Boasts a stabiliser and delivers incredibly sharp results.

Nikon AF-S 60mm f/2.8G ED Micro
Compact and light. Quiet and fast AF, and superb optics.

Sigma 50mm f/2.8 EX DG
Ideal for APS-C DSLRs. Has a minimum aperture of f/45.

Sigma 150mm f/2.8 EX DG OS HSM APO
A popular choice with enthusiasts and pros. Sports a stabiliser.

Tamron 60mm f/2 Di II Fast f/2 aperture delivers high-quality results with APS-C camera.

Tamron 90mm f/2.8
A classic lens. This version offers excellent optics and great handling.

Close-up filters

For beginners, this is the most affordable and simplest way to try out close-up photography

THE EASIEST, MOST affordable entry route to shooting miniature subjects is by using close-up filters – or supplementary close-up lenses as they are technically known (because they don't filter anything). These are circular, screw-in type filters that act like reading glasses for your camera, reducing the lens's minimum focusing distance. By doing so, they are able to transform a normal lens into one with a better close-focusing ability. They are lightweight and don't affect the camera's automatic functions (like metering and autofocus) or reduce the amount of light entering the lens. They couldn't be easier to use, either – simply screw one onto the front of your lens and you are ready to shoot close-ups. Costing as little as £10 for a set of three strengths of magnification (measured in dioptres: a unit you might be familiar with from visits to an optician), they are perfectly suited to beginners and photographers on a budget. Most major filter brands have close-up filters in their range, so there is no shortage of choice.

They work by shifting the camera's plane of focus from infinity to the distance corresponding to the focal length of the close-up lens attached. They are convex meniscus-type lenses – thicker in the middle than at the edges – and most close-up filters are a single element construction. They are available in a range of strengths, typically +1, +2, +3 and +4. The higher the number, the greater their magnification. Powerful +10 versions are also available. They can be purchased singly or as a set and, generally speaking, are best used with short telephoto lengths, in the region of 50mm to 135mm. However, they also work well with zooms, too. They are suitable for all types of subjects, from still-lifes to nature. However, they don't provide a large working distance, so be prepared to have to get very close to your subject to capture frame-filling shots.

The pros & cons...

✔ Easy to use
✔ Inexpensive
✔ No reduction in light
✔ Retain camera's auto functions
✔ Lightweight and portable
✘ Not the best image quality
✘ Results can suffer from spherical and chromatic aberration
✘ Short working distance

Helpful hints

1) Close-up filters are available in different filter threads, with the most common sizes being 49mm, 52mm, 58mm and 67mm. Remember to check the size you need before buying.
2) Instead of buying several dioptres of different sizes to fit the different diameter lenses in your system, consider 'buying big' and using 'step-up' rings so that one filter will fit all. Step-up rings are designed to adapt a filter to a lens when the two have different diameters: both saving money and conserving space in your camera bag.
3) For best image quality, use lens apertures of f/5.6 and above. This reduces aberrations inherent to such simple optics and also increases depth-of-field usefully, though will make shutter speeds longer, so be wary of camera shake!

Using close-up filters

Close-up filters couldn't be simpler to use – screw one on to the filter thread of your camera's lens and it reduces its minimum focusing distance. However, it is useful to be able to calculate the level of magnification achieved by any given lens and close-up filter combination. To do this, you'll need to be prepared to do a little arithmetic – so if maths wasn't your strong point at school, now's the time to reach for your calculator.

First, establish what the dioptre's equivalent value is in millimetres. To do this, divide 1,000 by the strength of the dioptre. For example, to calculate the value of a +4 dioptre: 1,000 / 4 = 250mm. Next, divide the focal length of the lens in millimetres by the equivalent focal length of the filter. So, for instance, if you were to attach a +4 dioptre to a 50mm prime lens, this would achieve a magnification of: 50 / 250 = 0.2x – approximately 1:5. So, the equation you need to remember is: magnification = focal length of lens / focal length of dioptre. However, this calculation only reveals the magnification of the lens when it is focused on infinity: even greater levels of magnification are possible when the lens is set to a shorter focusing distance.

It's possible to combine close-up filters to achieve even higher levels of magnification – for example, coupling a +1 and +2 filter together achieves a level of magnification equivalent to a +3 dioptre. However, if you do this, always attach the most powerful first and the weakest last, as this maximises image quality. Avoid coupling three or more close-up filters together, as this will significantly degrade image quality and exaggerate any optical flaws.

While there are many advantages to using close-up filters, they cannot compete with the image quality of other close-up attachments – which is hardly surprising, considering their low price tag and basic construction. Edge sharpness in particular can suffer, and they are prone to ghosting and spherical and chromatic aberration. However, you can maximise image quality by selecting an aperture of f/5.6 or higher, and only combining them with the better quality optics – for example, prime, fixed focal lengths.

Opting for higher quality filters, with two elements (doublet construction) is another option. However, expect to pay upwards of £80 for one.

Gribbit a go!
Close-up filters may not match a macro lens for sharpness, often noticeable around the edges, but they're a brilliant budget introduction to close-ups.

No filter

+2

+4

+10

Extension tubes

Get up close and personal with extension tubes – an excellent budget macro option capable of brilliant results…

IF YOU CAN'T justify buying a dedicated macro lens, but don't want to compromise image quality by using close-up filters, consider investing in a set of auto extension tubes. These hollow tubes fit between camera and lens in order to extend the lens further away from the sensor plane. By doing so, they reduce the lens's minimum focusing distance, allowing you to focus closer and achieve a greater level of subject magnification. They are available in different camera mount fittings and, as they are constructed without any optical elements, image quality is good. However, they do reduce the amount of light entering the camera: the higher the magnification, the more light lost. Your camera's TTL metering will automatically compensate for this reduction, but shutter speeds will lengthen as a result of using one: an important consideration if you intend shooting handheld.

Auto extension tubes are compact, light and, combined with a good quality lens, are capable of producing excellent results, comparable to that of a macro lens. They can be bought individually or in sets. Most are 12/20/36mm including Kenko's (illustrated): the longer the tube, the larger the reproduction ratio. They can also be used together to generate higher levels of magnification, equal to or exceeding 1:1 (life-size). Overall, they are a very versatile and useful close-up attachment.

Non-automatic versions are available and are typically quite cheap to buy. However, they disable many of the camera's key automatic functions, like metering and focusing, so you need to take more care when using them. Auto extension tubes cost from around £100 and retain all the metering and focusing connections, making them convenient and simple to use. Their biggest restriction is that, like close-up filters, working distances tend to be short, making it difficult

to position additional light sources and increasing the risk of frightening away live subjects. However, they are well-suited to most close-up subjects and are a useful attachment to have in your camera bag, being handy for reducing the minimum focusing distance of longer lenses, too.

The pros & cons…

✔ With no optical elements, good image quality is maintained

✔ Light and easy to carry

✔ Affordable

✔ Simple to use

✔ Useful for reducing the minimum focusing distance of longer lenses

✘ Reduces light entering the camera: the greater the magnification, the more light lost

✘ Short working distance

✘ Non-automatic versions disable camera functions, like metering and autofocus

✘ More fiddly than macro lenses

Extension tubes: Frequently asked questions

Q What are the best lenses to use with auto extension tubes?
A If you want images with a high magnification, extension tubes are best combined with short focal lengths – a lens in the region of 35mm to 100mm is ideal. Small amounts of extension, like 12mm, are most effective coupled with short focal lengths, like 35mm or 50mm. The amount of extension you require will greatly depend on the size of the subject and the level of magnification desired. While extension tubes can be useful with any focal length in order to reduce its minimum focusing distance, achieving high reproduction ratios using focal lengths exceeding 100mm is usually impractical: the amount of extension required is too great, resulting in too much light being lost.

Q How do I fit auto extension tubes to my camera outfit?
A Attaching and using auto extension tubes couldn't be easier. With the camera switched off, remove the body cap. Next, attach the extension tube as you would a lens: aligning the indicators marked on the tube and camera mount, and then rotating it (in the correct orientation) until the tube clicks into position. Next, attach the lens, aligning the indicators on the tube and lens, and then rotating the lens until it clicks into position. Auto extension tubes are constructed with contacts to enable automatic metering and focusing. Therefore, when you switch the camera on, the camera and lens will function normally and you are ready to begin taking close-ups.

Magnification

The magnification achieved using extension tubes varies depending on the length of the tube and focal length of the lens. However, approximating the reproduction ratio of any given tube and lens combination is fairly simple: just divide the amount of extension by the focal length of the lens. For example, if you combine a 25mm extension tube with a 50mm lens, the magnification is 25 / 50 = 0.5x or 1:2 (half life-size). Using the same level of extension with a 100mm lens would result in a reproduction ratio of 1:4 (quarter life-size). If you want to achieve a level of magnification equal to 1:1 (life-size), you need to employ a level of extension equal to that of the focal length of the lens – for example, 50mm of extension with a 50mm lens. See the quick reference chart (right) for the level

Extension	35mm	50mm	100mm
12mm	0.34x (1:2.9)	0.24x (1:4.1)	0.12x (1:8.3)
25mm	**0.71x (1:1.4)**	**0.5x (1:2)**	**0.25x (1:4)**
36mm	1.03x (1:0.97)	0.72x (1:1.3)	0.36x (1:2.7)

of magnification achieved using extension tubes with three popular focal lengths. As you can see, the shorter the focal length, the greater the magnification.

Comparison set (right): This set of images shows the major difference in magnification using 12mm, 25mm and 36mm auto extension tubes when combined with a standard 50mm lens.

Reversing your lens

This option offers the highest magnification of all macro accessories, but requires a bit of extra effort for you to gain the best results. Here's everything you need to know about reversing rings…

REVERSING RINGS ARE a useful close-up attachment. They are capable of high magnifications, exceeding that of the others featured on the previous pages. Reversing rings work by allowing a lens to be mounted back to front on the camera. This adaptor is designed with a rear lens mount one side and a male filter thread on the other, allowing the lens to attach to the body. By reversing a lens in this way, its optical centre is displaced from the sensor plane, introducing a level of extension and enabling it to focus much closer.

The exact level of magnification depends on the focal length of the lens and level of displacement. The shorter the lens, the higher the magnification. A prime lens is generally considered best, while a focal length in the region of 28mm to 50mm is a popular choice. Magnifications exceeding twice life-size are possible using reversing rings, although expect the subject-to-camera distance to be no more than a few millimetres at high reproduction ratios.

You may be wondering how optical quality isn't greatly degraded by being reversed. Well, to maintain the highest image quality, a lens should have its largest element facing the longest distance. Normally, the distance between camera and subject is much larger than the one between lens and sensor. However, when working so close to the subject, the opposite can be true. As a result, having the front element of the lens reversed helps to ensure high image quality.

At extremely high reproduction ratios, it is best to stay in the confines of indoors, or a controlled studio environment, until you gain experience. Depth-of-field will prove exceptionally shallow and lighting will be severely restricted. At less extreme magnifications, it is suitable for a wide variety of close-up subjects – indoors or out. However, due to their short working distance, keep to static subjects and use a tripod to aid stability and focusing.

Pros & cons…

- ✔ Excellent image quality
- ✔ High magnifications of 1:1 and higher are possible
- ✘ Very short working distance
- ✘ Automatic versions are expensive

Your choice of manual or auto rings

It is possible to buy manual or automatic reversing rings. In fact, manual versions are one of the cheapest close-up attachments, costing as little as £10. However, before you rush out and order one, it is important to realise that automatic metering and focusing will be lost and some lenses will require another adaptor to control the lens diaphragm so you can change apertures.

The best lenses for use with manual rings are those lenses that feature an aperture ring: Pentax and older Nikon lenses, for instance, and also manual-focus Olympus OM and Canon FD lenses. Check the secondhand shelves of local dealers and you should find them at affordable prices. For ease of use and speed, a dedicated auto reversing ring, like the Novoflex EOS-RETRO (www.speedgraphic.co.uk), is a

far better option. With these, one end attaches to a camera mount and the other to the rear mount of the lens, with a flex lead maintaining electronic communication between the two. A filter ring is screwed into the filter thread of the lens and is used to attach the front of the lens to the camera-mount unit. Step-down rings (see below left) can be used to connect lenses with a wider filter thread to the lens mount unit.

Autofocus and metering is possible, but bear in mind that, at such close distances, manual focus is usually better. These specialist auto rings aren't cheap, costing around £250, but they do allow for incredibly large, striking close-up images.

Stepping rings

Stepping rings are designed to adapt a filter to a lens when the two have differing filter thread diameters. For example, if you own a 72mm filter, but wish to use it in combination with a 67mm thread-fit lens, a suitable step-up ring would allow you to do this. They are made from either metal or plastic, are relatively cheap and available in a wide range of sizes. There are two types of step rings – step-up and step-down. Step-up rings are a handy and cost effective way to expand the compatibility and usefulness of larger filters. Step-down rings are generally less practical as, due to their nature, they enhance the risk of vignetting. But they are useful to attach a reversed lens with a larger filter thread to an auto ring. We used a Kood 77-58mm ring to fit the Canon EF 17-40mm f/4L to the Novoflex set-up.

Using an Auto ring set-up

Daniel Lezano tries out the Novoflex EOS-RETRO system

I've long enjoyed close-up photography and the 100mm macro is one of my favourite lenses. I've never tried reversing a lens and welcomed the chance to try out the Novoflex, as it retains electronic communication between the camera and body, greatly simplifying the picture-taking process as it allows the metering and AF functions to operate.

This gave the benefit of using aperture-priority mode with multi-zone metering and

would help reduce the challenges I would face. I used the Novoflex with a Canon EOS 550D and Canon 17-40mm f/4L lens. I discovered the autofocus struggled to lock on the subject due to the high magnification, so I found I focused manually most of the time. This wasn't a major concern, as I normally use manual focus with the 100mm.

The Novoflex lets you shoot at very high magnifications and so you need to be prepared to work patiently at capturing good images. The short working distance means you need to get

THOMAS SHAHAN

Larger than life
With experience and practice, you could shoot amazing close-ups like this with your reversed lens set-up.

very close to your subject and so when shooting bugs, as I was, expect many to have flown or crawled off by the time you're ready to shoot.

At such high magnification, you physically need to move forwards and backwards until the subject starts to appear in focus. I had my set-up mounted on a Manfrotto 190XPROB (you are advised to tripod-mount your set-up due to the severe risk of shake), so it meant sliding the entire set-up to and fro. I found it quickest to start with the zoom at the tele-setting (ie 40mm) and the manual focus set to a

mid-focus distance. I would then move the set-up until the subject appeared reasonably sharp, then fine-tune the focus. If I wanted to magnify the subject further, I would zoom the lens towards its wide-angle end (sounds odd, but this is correct!) and adjust the focus again.

It's a slow process, but it worked. Two final bits of advice: try to get the sensor plane parallel to the subject as depth-of-field is incredibly shallow. And if you can use LiveView, do so, as it makes focusing and composition so much easier and quicker.

`Set-up`

You need to get very close to your subject to achieve the best possible magnification. This spider was only around 5mm long. Note the shallow depth-of-field that was achieved.

WildFlowers

Nature is one of the most popular subjects to photograph; it is also one of the most technically challenging. Here, award-winning natural history photographer Ross Hoddinott exclusively shares his knowledge of capturing great images of the wild plants that burst into flower along our hedgerows and woodlands ⊙

OUR MEADOWLAND, hedgerows and woodland are brimming with colour come the summer. Wild flowers reach their annual peak, presenting photographers with countless opportunities to capture stunning floral images. They can literally spring up anywhere, growing along roadside verges and even appearing between cracks in pavements, so regardless of where you live, you shouldn't need to venture far to find flowering plants to snap. They can be shot using practically any focal length; a wide-angle can be used to photograph them in context with their surroundings, a zoom or telephoto to shoot small groups and a macro or close-up attachment to isolate individual flowers. As a result, regardless of your kit and budget, great shots are within your grasp.

The size, shape, colour and form of our native wild plants varies tremendously, making it tricky to give specific advice on how best to photograph them. To a great extent, the subject, its environment and the light will dictate your approach. However, I guarantee your wild flower images will benefit from my tried-and-tested tips and guidelines.

Gear up!

To photograph wild flowers, you ideally need a macro lens or close-up attachment. If you can't justify the cost of a dedicated macro, consider using either extension tubes or a close-up filter combined with a standard focal length. A telephoto – in the region of 200mm to 300mm – is useful for shooting larger flowers, like orchids. Also, a wide-angle lens can prove handy if you wish to photograph carpets of flowers or images including the subject's surroundings. Always carry a sturdy tripod to avoid camera shake and aid composition, although if you're shooting from ground level, a beanbag will prove more practical – along with a groundsheet to lay on. A reflector is another 'must-have' accessory. An atomiser (water spray bottle) can be employed to add fine, dew-like, water droplets. A polarising filter is useful to reduce reflective glare from foliage and a soft-focus filter can work well in combination with backlit subjects. An angle-finder is ideally suited to shooting wild flowers at ground level. Always focus manually for precision, unless your eyesight won't permit. Also, if your camera has a depth-of-field preview button, use it to check your selected aperture has generated sufficient depth-of-field. Release the shutter using the camera's self-timer to minimise camera movement.

Without reflector

With reflector

1 Using a reflector When photographing wild flowers, I only employ a burst of flash when the fastest available shutter speed remains too slow to freeze movement. Personally, I feel flash ruins an image's natural feel – destroying subtle colouring and fine detail. Instead, when the lighting is poor, I prefer to manipulate the natural light available. This is possible with the use of a reflector, such as the collapsible, lightweight types made by Lastolite. Alternatively, it is possible to make one by stretching kitchen foil over a piece of cardboard. A reflector couldn't be easier to use. Simply position it near to your subject and angle to direct natural light onto the area required. The intensity of the 'bounced'

light can be increased or lessened by moving the reflector closer or further away from the subject. While an essential aid when it's overcast or while taking pictures in woodland under a thick canopy of leaves, a reflector is also useful in bright, sunny conditions. For example, overhead sunlight will create ugly, harsh shadows that can be lifted by bouncing light onto the shaded regions. A reflector can prove fiddly and awkward to accurately position while taking pictures. Personally, I use a Wimberley Plamp to position my reflector. This is a ball-and-socket segmented arm with a clamp at either end. One end can be attached to a tripod leg, while the other holds the reflector.

2 Gardening Gardening is an essential part of wild-flower photography. Don't worry, though; you don't need green fingers. Gardening is a term given to the selective removal of grasses and other distracting elements from the foreground and background of the frame. Rarely, in my experience, will you photograph a plant in the wild without having to do some degree of tidying first – unless the subject is filling the viewfinder. The extent you have to garden depends on the environment and f/stop employed. At wide apertures, depth-of-field is shallow, so less tidying is required as the subject's background quickly drifts out of focus. In contrast, when using narrow apertures, the extended depth-of-field created retains more detail and definition in the subject's surroundings – making gardening a more fiddly, time-consuming process.

Before

While minor background distractions can be later removed using the Clone Tool in Photoshop, others cannot, without it being obvious in the final image. It is far better to get the image right in-camera. My approach is to first compose the image and set the exposure. I then preview the depth-of-field, carefully studying the frame to identify anything that might prove distracting. If your SLR lacks a preview facility, take a shot and scrutinise it on the LCD monitor. I then carefully flatten them with my hand or use scissors to remove them. This should be done with care and consideration. Only remove grasses, etc; never cut or destroy other wild flowers. Ultimately, you are striving for a clean and diffused background.

Aesthetically, the difference between a gardened and non-gardened image can be striking. While selective tidying might slow down the picture-taking process, unlike other natural-history subjects, wild flowers are not going to move or fly away. Therefore, there's no need to rush. Remember; what you exclude from the frame can often prove as important as what you actually include. ➔

"Rarely, in my experience, will you photograph a plant in the wild without having to do some degree of tidying first"

After gardening
Taking a few moments to tidy up your composition before triggering the shutter can make the difference between an average image and one that really stands out. Your subject isn't going anywhere, so take your time and get it right.

3 **Lighting** As with any subject, lighting is a key area and the way in which you use ambient light greatly dictates the look of the final image. I often prefer to work on bright, but overcast days. Foliage glare is reduced, colours are more saturated and the lower contrast allows me to capture fine detail that might otherwise be washed out. However, shutter speeds are lengthened in overcast conditions, so a still day is required and a camera support essential. Side or frontal light is fine, but avoid shooting around midday when the overhead sun is harsh. If unavoidable, cast your shadow across the subject to lower contrast and use a tripod and self-timer to trigger the shutter.

To capture wild-flower images with more drama and impact, backlight it. Evening or morning light is best, when the sun is low in the sky and is perfect for highlighting shape and form. It can create wonderful results – illuminating tiny hairs and detail on stems, and giving petals a transparent appearance. To backlight a subject, you need to shoot into the direction of the light, so there is the risk of lens flare. To avoid this problem, use a lens hood or shield it with your hand or a piece of card. The tricky lighting conditions can easily deceive metering systems, so check images via the LCD and bracket exposure settings.

4 **Depth-of-field** The aperture you select, and the resulting depth-of-field, will greatly dictate the look and feel of the final image. There is no definitive rule regarding how much, or how little, depth-of-field is required; this is a decision you need to make at the time of taking the picture, based on the effect you wish to achieve. If you want to draw the eye of the viewer to a specific point of focus, use a wide aperture, like f/2.8 or f/4. If you want to maximise back-to-front sharpness, opt for a high f/number, like f/16 or f/22. Your camera cannot predict the effect you desire, so it is important to set apertures manually, rather than rely on one of your camera's automated exposure modes. If you are unsure which aperture will create the best effect, why not simply take a sequence of images with different f/numbers and decide later which you prefer? I did this when I photographed this close-up of a celandine flower. In this instance, I much prefer the images taken with a shallow depth-of-field.

Common wild flowers

Here are five of the most popular wild flowers to photograph in the UK.

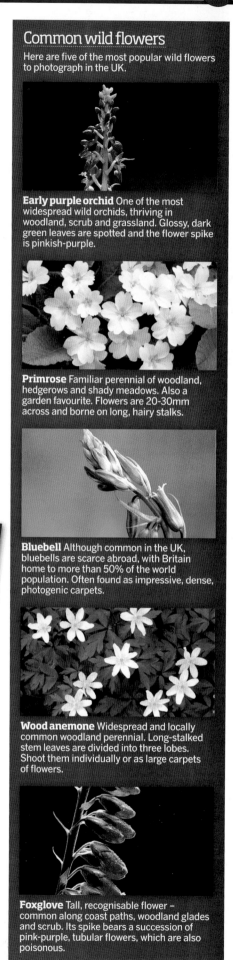

Early purple orchid One of the most widespread wild orchids, thriving in woodland, scrub and grassland. Glossy, dark green leaves are spotted and the flower spike is pinkish-purple.

Primrose Familiar perennial of woodland, hedgerows and shady meadows. Also a garden favourite. Flowers are 20-30mm across and borne on long, hairy stalks.

Bluebell Although common in the UK, bluebells are scarce abroad, with Britain home to more than 50% of the world population. Often found as impressive, dense, photogenic carpets.

Wood anemone Widespread and locally common woodland perennial. Long-stalked stem leaves are divided into three lobes. Shoot them individually or as large carpets of flowers.

Foxglove Tall, recognisable flower – common along coast paths, woodland glades and scrub. Its spike bears a succession of pink-purple, tubular flowers, which are also poisonous.

5 Originality Producing fresh images of common, well-photographed flora is far from easy and too often we record a subject in a certain style or way, simply through habit. In other words, preconceived ideas can stifle our creativity. Digital capture has made it easier than ever to experiment, so be imaginative. Each species has the potential to be shot in an infinite number of ways. It is possible to produce a varied set of images from the same subject by simply altering the viewpoint, focal length, lighting, exposure, background or camera-to-subject distance. Each parameter can have a dramatic effect over the look and feel of the final image. In my experience, it is best to begin by taking the image that is immediately most obvious, then move around the subject and consider different approaches. Try shooting from low and high viewpoints, then vary focal lengths and depth-of-field. Fill the frame with the flower, but also take a shot showing it small in its environment. If it is breezy, use a long shutter speed to deliberately blur the flower. The possibilities are only limited by your imagination. Here, I visited a local woodland where wood anemones grow in large numbers and captured these very different results within minutes.

Original

Water droplets

Adding water droplets can give visual interest to flower images – it's easy when you know how

Daniel Lezano With so much rain falling in the UK, especially in the last couple of years, producing a guide to mimicking raindrops could be deemed a little odd. Unfortunately, most of our rain falls during the colder months when garden flowers are sparse, so with fewer showers during the summer, the only way to photograph raindrops is to create them ourselves.

This can easily be done using a water spray bottle, a watering can or garden hose. If you're using one of the latter two options, be sure that the nozzle has an attachment that sprays water, rather than one that provides a heavy stream that could damage delicate plants.

There are a number of different ways that droplets can settle on garden foliage, each providing the opportunity for a different type of image. One of the most popular is capturing droplets hanging off a stem, usually in groups of two or three. This is an effective technique that has an added dimension if there are flowers nearby that can be refracted in the droplets, as seen in the image above. If you want to try this technique, choose a viewpoint that takes the backdrop into account. The other favoured image is a far simpler one, but equally pleasing, and requires you to cover the surface of a leaf or petals with dozens of small droplets by spraying them with water.

Refraction in droplets
Fancy trying out this alternative approach? Turn the page over to find out how!

For this step-by-step, I wanted to try a technique that I'd not seen before and that was to create a single droplet that rested on a flower, rather than hanging from it. My chosen flower was a purple allium, one of my favourites to photograph due to the intricate nature of its multi-flowered bloom. As I'll be moving around trying different angles, I'm shooting handheld and using a 100mm macro lens to help me get close. The bright sunlight means avoiding camera shake won't be a problem, but the odd breeze means I need to keep shutter speeds relatively high to avoid blur caused by the subject's movement during the exposure. I use aperture-priority mode as I want to retain close control of depth-of-field.

One final point: droplets tend to form more easily and hold their cohesion better on humid days when there is more moisture in the air. Therefore, if a summer storm is brewing, head into the garden and you'll find this technique easier to achieve than on hot, dry days.

1 Apply the water Try applying a light dusting of water on the flower using a spray to see the effect it has. Unfortunately, on this type of flower, I find the spread of water is good, but the droplets are too small and not large enough in the frame. I need to find an alternative!

2 Experiment I try using a hose, but the result is the same. I decide I need to apply a larger drop with more control and attempt to do this using a straw dipped into a jar of water. By using my finger on the end of the straw, I do my best to control the release of water onto the allium.

3 Keep trying It takes a few attempts, but I eventually manage to settle a large droplet of water on a flower. It's proof that with a little patience and luck, the straw method can work. This particular droplet is too large, so I shake the allium and keep trying until I manage to do better.

4 Find your viewpoint It takes a few more attempts, but I have a droplet that is a more suitable size. Now it's a case of trying to find a good viewpoint and the best aperture setting. I start by shooting from above, but the result is flat, so I shift my position and look for alternatives.

5 Get eye-level with the subject Adopting a lower viewpoint gives the image more three-dimensionality and the droplet is clearly visible due to the shallow depth-of-field. However, the out-of-focus foreground is distracting and the dark backdrop is unattractive.

Final image
By shifting my position slightly higher, I've made a dramatic improvement to the composition. Not only does the subject now dominate the frame, the foreground is less cluttered and the green vegetation in the background is far more appealing. The aperture of f/8 provides the perfect amount of depth-of-field, too.

Shoot a colourful flower refracted in water droplets

There's a reason why photographers love this technique – it's great fun to do and the results are always interesting

Ross Hoddinott: You could argue that photographing the refracted image of a colourful flower through one or more water droplets hanging on a stem or branch is a bit of a cliché, and with some justification, too. However, while it may not be the most original idea, there is no denying that the results can look eye-catching. Because it has been done many times before, it is easy to overlook taking this type of shot. This is a mistake, though. There is nothing wrong with replicating an idea – so long as you do it well, and enjoy the challenge of achieving the final result. ➔

Set up: This type of image is easy to shoot and should take no more than an hour. You can set up in your garden or indoors, using a small table as your base. A macro lens would be the ideal choice, as they typically have a 1:1 reproduction ratio, but a reversing ring, close-up lens or extension tube would also work. A remote release will also be useful (or, if you don't have one, your camera's self-timer will help), as will a small reflector. You'll need a colourful flower to photograph, such as a gerbera or sunflower.

The flower and the object your droplets are hanging from need to be clamped into position, and the droplets should be suspended between 10-30cm in front of the flower, from a thin reed, grass or branch. Wimberley Plamps are useful for this, but bulldog clips or tape will also work. Lastly, to create your droplets, use a water sprayer or atomiser. Spray repeatedly until large droplets form and hang from your reed or branch. This can be a rather frustrating process, so it may take a few attempts to get the droplets just right.

Recommended kit

Wimberley Plamp:
I'm using a basic tabletop set-up and have bought a large, red gerbera from the local florist. The bigger the flower, the better, as it will also be the backdrop for the shot. My droplets are suspended from a fresh green reed, from my pond. I attach two Wimberley Plamps to the table; one to hold the reed in place and the other to position the flower around 20cm behind. The reed needs to be held horizontally otherwise the water will run along it, but the advantage of using 'Plamps' is that their flexible arms are easy to adjust and position. I align the flower and reed so that the flower head creates a frame-filling backdrop. Next, I spray the reed with an atomiser until a row of droplets form. Having done this, I move my tripod into position – parallel to the droplets and flower behind.

1 Take a test shot Just by looking at the row of droplets, I can see the perfect miniature refracted image of the flower in every drop. I decide to focus on a couple of droplets that are side by side. Next, I prioritise a large aperture of f/4 in order to throw the flower behind completely out of focus. I then focus on the droplets and release the shutter. However, by focusing on the drop itself, rather than the refraction, the flower images are out of focus.

2 Adjust focus With close-up photography, depth-of-field is often just a matter of millimetres. Therefore, accurate focusing is critical, which is why if your eyesight allows it, you should always opt for the added precision of manual focus. I carefully alter my point of focus, so that it is on the refracted image of the flower. However, depth-of-field is so narrow at f/4, that nothing other than my point of focus is recorded as acceptably sharp.

Final image
Experiment with vertical and horizontal compositions and alter the shooting angle. I try several approaches, including this one where each drop is in focus. But my favourite image is the one on the previous page where I opt for a composition at a slight angle to the reed, focusing on a single droplet, keeping the flower within it sharp, while everything else drifts pleasantly out of focus.

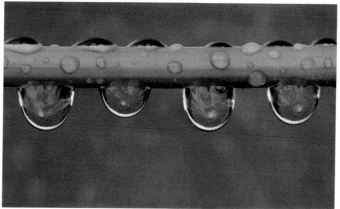

3 Use a smaller aperture In aperture-priority mode, I select a smaller f/number of f/14. I hope this will generate enough depth-of-field to keep the droplets, refracted images and reed in acceptable focus. The resulting slower shutter speed increases the risk of camera shake, so even the tiniest vibration caused by pressing the shutter release button will soften the image. Therefore, the use of a remote release is essential to ensure a sharp result.

4 Create more drops The previous image is okay, but the composition isn't terribly exciting. I decide that isolating just two of the droplets doesn't create a strong enough visual impact, so I spray the reeds again to create more drops, and then focus on a larger group. I maintain the settings for the last image, using f/14 with a corresponding shutter speed of 1/4sec. The result is more interesting, but I am certain that I can do better.

Weeds, glorious weeds...

Unwanted weedy visitors to your garden look a lot better on camera than they do in your lawn!

Daniel Lezano: Unless you've someone in your home who's totally dedicated to their garden, chances are there are areas where weeds make an unwelcome appearance. Normally, that calls for a small trowel to dig them up and a dose of weedkiller. However, the dandelion is one weed that photographers should look forward to seeing as it makes for very photogenic images. Rather than the actual flower, it's the dandelion clock, also known as a parachute ball, that deserves your attention. This delicate head is made up of small, lightweight seeds that break apart from the clock and float off with the breeze. This makes them beautiful but difficult to handle, so while it's possible to pluck one and move it into a suitable location, you'll often find it's best to shoot it where it has grown.

There are various ways you can photograph a dandelion clock, so it's worth trying out as many as you can before it breaks up. One of the most popular is to adopt a low angle and shoot it against a dark backdrop or a blue sky, polarised to boost the contrast. Another is to fire a sequence of images while some seeds are blown off the head, so that they are caught in mid-air, then shooting the clock with its remainder of seeds.

All these ideas are worth trying but for this step-by-step, I've decided to shoot something a little different to the other garden images in this guide.

Instead of going for a colourful image of the clock, I'll be looking to produce a more detailed, monotone and abstract result. I've set up my camera with a 100mm macro lens on a Manfrotto 190XPROB, which has a useful collar that allows the centre column to be quickly adjusted for low-level shooting. It's a bright day, so I set a low ISO of 100, and with aperture-priority mode selected, I shoot each frame at f/5.6, f/8 and f/11 to vary the depth-of-field – I'll decide later which I prefer. As focusing is critical, I set single-point AF to ensure I focus on the centre of the clock.

In situ

Reflector cover

Diffuser

Set-up 1

Set-up 2

Set-up 3

1 Find your subject Dandelions are one of the most common garden weeds, so you shouldn't have much trouble finding a suitable crop. I discovered one growing through some gravel beside my shed (the wife won't be happy!). Here's a 'straight' shot taken of the dandelion clock to show it in its natural setting. The green and brown backdrop is not particularly inspiring, so some measures need to be taken to improve the result.

2 Dial in exposure compensation I place the black cover of my reflector behind the dandelion clock and it's an instant improvement, with the white head standing out from the backdrop. I need to dial in -1EV exposure compensation to prevent the clock losing detail – check exposures via your LCD monitor. While better, the result is still too bland. To reveal the intricacies of the clock, I need to work out a way to shoot the subject backlit.

3 Introduce diffuser The solution is easy – I place the diffuser of my 5-in-1 reflector behind the dandelion clock (a sheet of white paper or net curtain can also be used if you don't have a diffuser panel). Due to the low angle, I shoot handheld, using the tripod to support the diffuser. The image is instantly much better than previous attempts. The bright sunlight gives a near-white backdrop and the dandelion clock is recorded as a near-silhouette.

Wonderful weed

A quick tweak in Levels (*Image>Adjustment>Levels*) to improve the contrast of the silhouette effect, followed by the addition of a slight tint using *Image>Adjustments>Hue/Saturation*... and I'm done.

Magic mushrooms!

Autumn brings the chance to capture lovely shots of fungi. Follow these tips to bring out their true beauty

Ross Hoddinott: For this step-by-step, you'll need the right conditions before you head out with your camera – notably shorter days, a leaf-laden woodland floor and a distinct autumn chill! Autumn is a wonderful time of year for outdoor photography. As the weather turns cooler, photogenic mists hang in valleys and trees, and woodlands turn golden brown. This is also the season for photographing fungi. While they may not be considered the most exciting or glamorous subjects, toadstools and mushrooms are highly photogenic. There are thousands of types, ranging greatly in colour, size, shape and design. Fungi can grow practically anywhere, from parks to garden lawns. However, many species enjoy damp, mature woodland, where there are fallen trunks, mossy stumps and deep leaf litter. October and November are the best times to visit your local woodland in search of fungi. This is a subject accessible to all photographers, with only a basic set-up required. Naturally, you will need a digital SLR – preferably with LiveView – and also a macro lens or close-up attachment, such as extension tubes or close-up filters. Fungi enjoy growing in dark environments, so the stability of a tripod is essential and also a reflector or flashgun to help illuminate your subject.

1 Find your subject I visit a local wood, which I know is good for fungi during autumn. After searching for ten minutes, I find a stump with an attractive group of mushrooms growing from it. They are in pristine condition and in a good position for photography. I attach my DSLR to a tripod and take a picture. However, the messy surroundings and overhanging ivy are distracting.

2 Be prepared to 'garden' within your frame You have to pay particular attention to your subject's surroundings when shooting close-ups. I always keep scissors in my backpack to tidy up the frame – a technique known to photographers as 'gardening'. I remove the surrounding ivy, but am very careful not to damage the fungi.

3 Take a test shot To eliminate the problem of the distracting background, I opt to move my tripod slightly closer to try a tight composition. The result is an improvement, but the parallel viewpoint is rather uninteresting and, overall, the shot lacks impact. The parallel viewpoint may work with some subjects, but in this case it clearly doesn't do the job.

☑ Be prepared!
To avoid getting damp, muddy clothing, wear waterproof trousers or carry a groundsheet or bin liner to kneel on

4 Change viewpoint The intricacy and pattern of a mushroom's gills is usually the most photogenic and interesting feature. Therefore, low viewpoints, looking upwards, often produce the best images. Next, I reposition my tripod, but due to the low, awkward angle, I am struggling to compose the image accurately and comfortably through my DSLR's viewfinder.

5 Use LiveView When shooting at low, awkward angles, LiveView is a really helpful feature. I switch on LiveView and using the screen, I compose the shot without having to contort my body. The low angle really emphasises the fungi's gills, creating a more interesting shot. DSLRs with a vari-angle LCD monitor are even better adapted for this type of photography.

Final image
A mushroom image that's truly magic. Why don't you head out to the woods and give this technique a try?

Essential kit

When photographing fungi in dark woodland, the light is often limited. This, combined with the fact that you will often want to select a high f/number in the region of f/16 or f/22 (to generate sufficient depth-of-field), means shutter speeds are typically slow. To ensure pin-sharp images, a tripod and remote release are essential. If the woodland floor is damp and soft, push the tripod feet into the ground for extra security. Even when using a tripod, physically pressing the shutter release button can cause small vibrations that soften images, so fire the shutter remotely using a remote release or the camera's self-timer function. If your camera has a 'mirror-lock' function, use it. This locks up the reflex mirror before releasing the shutter, eliminating internal vibrations.

6 Try fill-flash The disadvantage of using a low viewpoint is that the underneath of the fungi is in dark shadow, obscuring detail and proving quite ugly – especially as light levels in a dense woodland can be quite low to start with. A burst of fill-flash can be used to relieve this, but it can prove too harsh and unnatural in such close proximity to the subject.

7 Introduce a reflector I prefer to use a reflector. You can instantly see its effect on the subject and alter the light's intensity by moving it closer or tilting the angle. It's the most natural-looking way to illuminate miniature subjects, and the simplest. Holding the reflector close, I bounce light back up on to the fungi and release the shutter again. Finally, a fungi image to be proud of.

Insects

Nature is one of the most popular subjects to photograph, as well as being one of the most technically challenging. In this section, award-winning natural history photographer *Ross Hoddinott* shares his expert knowledge of photographing nature, from finding great subjects to taking your finest shots of them… ➔

BUGS AND CREEPY crawlies do not have a good reputation, do they? Despite their tiny size, they seem to strike terror among people. However, if you're 'brave' enough to take a closer look, you'll discover that the majority of them are colourful, intricately formed and very photogenic. In the UK, few insects bite or sting, so it's an irrational fear. Therefore, rather than run away, photographers should put their phobias aside and reach for their camera instead…

Some of the techniques and principles outlined in the *Wild Flowers* masterclass on pages 54-59 can also be applied to photographing insects – for example, the importance of lighting, originality and the need for 'gardening'. However, the mobility, size and timid nature of mini beasts present photographers with a fresh set of practical and technical dilemmas. Firstly, you need to identify a suitable habitat where you'll find them. Wildlife photographers often need to research their subjects before they begin snapping, so visit your local library or surf the internet for information.

Gear up for creepy crawlies!

To photograph insects, you'll need a macro lens or close-up attachment. If your budget can stretch to it, a dedicated macro lens is a great investment, allowing a practical working distance from which to take pictures. A lens in the region of 100-180mm is traditionally best for snapping insects. However, if you are a beginner, student or have a limited budget, try using extension tubes or a close-up lens/dioptre in combination with a standard focal length. Both accessories are comparatively inexpensive and provide a good introduction to the world of close-ups. A 70-300mm zoom with close focusing can sometimes be used to snap larger insects like dragonflies. If the insect is resting, a reflector may be used to bounce light onto the subject, so keep one in your camera bag. Due to the nature of insect photography, a tripod is often impractical. A monopod can prove a more practical form of support, but if you don't own one, simply keep the legs of your tripod closed together and use it as a makeshift monopod. Enthusiasts may wish to invest in a ring- or twin-flash unit. These dedicated macro accessories provide artificial illumination for close-up subjects when natural light is insufficient.

1 Get up early I won't try to pull the wool over your eyes: photographing insects is often challenging and full of frustration. For this reason, it's only logical to make life easier whenever possible. Insects are at their most lively during the warmth of mid-morning to late afternoon, so this time of day is best avoided whenever possible. It's better to shoot during the lower temperatures of morning and late evening, when their bodies are cold and they remain relatively inactive. So, if you're serious about capturing great insect shots, you need to set your alarm early…

During summer, you will need to drag yourself out of your warm, snug bed by 4.30am to be at your location by sunrise. Not fun I know, but the results will make it worthwhile. Look carefully amongst vegetation, tall grasses and leaves to find butterflies and bugs asleep. You will need a sharp eye, but with a little experience you will learn where to look. Tread carefully, though – a careless foot can prove fatal to these delicate, sleeping insects. One of the major advantages of photographing resting insects is that while they remain immobile, the area around them can be 'gardened' – see the *Wild Flowers* masterclass on pages 54-59. Also, after clear, dewy nights, tiny droplets of water will form on the insect's wings and body, adding scale and further interest.

2 Camera shake This is a common problem that occurs when the selected shutter speed isn't fast enough to eliminate your own natural movement, resulting in a blurry, ruined image. It's further exaggerated when using long focal lengths or high magnifications, so shake can prove a problem for insect photographers. The solution? Easy – just pop the camera on a tripod. Of course, it's often not that simple when shooting timid wildlife. While using a support is fine for many other forms of photography, a tripod is often impractical when photographing insects. For example, a flighty butterfly won't wait and pose for you while you try to set up your tripod. Insects are highly sensitive to movement and vibration, so if a tripod leg disturbs any surrounding grasses or vegetation near to the subject, it will soon scurry or fly off. In fact, in my experience, the only time a tripod is useful is during early morning or late evening when insects, like butterflies or damselflies, are asleep or settled for the arrival of night. At other times, you should be prepared to shoot handheld.

It's very easy to overestimate how steady you can hold a camera, but a good general rule for macro work is to employ a shutter speed at least double the focal length of the lens in use. Therefore, when using a 90mm macro, employ a shutter of at least 1/180sec. If your DSLR/lens has anti-shake technology, use it; sharp images can be produced at speeds two or three stops slower than without. Alternatively, to generate a faster shutter speed, employ a wider aperture (however, this will reduce depth-of-field) or increase your ISO rating. You can also limit the effects of shake through the way you support your camera. For example, kneeling is more stable than standing. Keep your elbows to your chest and hold the camera firmly to your face. Support the weight in your left hand and squeeze the shutter button smoothly. Your subject will often be low to the ground, so to achieve natural-looking results, lay prone to keep the camera parallel with the subject. This will also allow you to either use a beanbag or your elbows to steady your camera. Lying flat on the ground limits body movement, greatly reducing the risk of shake. ➔

Good support

Poor support

"If you're serious about capturing great insect shots, you need to set your alarm early"

Bugs before bedtime
If you're not an 'early bird', look for insects before sunset instead when they are preparing for overnight. The low, warm light at this time can be great for shooting insects, especially butterflies

✓ Turn off your beeps!
It's best to focus manually when snapping insects, but if you're using autofocus, then ensure that any noises or beeps that sound to indicate focusing are switched off before you start

3 Stalking Suitable insect-rich habitats can be found by researching a little on the internet, or by contacting a local wildlife organisation. However, locating potential subjects to shoot is the easy bit; getting near enough to photograph them can prove far trickier. Bugs are highly sensitive to movement, as they are constantly trying to avoid predation. As a result, they will quickly scurry or fly away unless you approach them with great care. 'Stalking' is a term nature photographers use to describe approaching wild animals to within photographic range – in a stealth-like manner. Having found a suitable subject, consider your approach. Note the position of the sun and begin moving nearer, doing so slowly and avoiding sudden or jerky movements, while being mindful of where your shadow is falling. If the subject is low to the ground, get down on your knees in advance and 'wriggle' forward. Admittedly, you will look rather silly to any onlookers, but it is a small price to pay for a great shot. When you get near, slowly bring the camera up to your eye while moving yourself into a shooting position. Take a frame from slightly further away to guarantee one shot 'in the bag' and help the creature get accustomed to the sound of your shutter. Still looking through the viewfinder, move closer again – refocusing as you do so – compose your shot and shoot. If the insect moves, try to keep it in sight. Some insects – for example, dragonflies and some butterflies – are territorial and, having flown away, may return to the same resting place a few moments later. Therefore, if you remain in position, you may well get a second chance.

4 Get your DSLR parallel At the high level of magnification required to shoot insects, depth-of-field grows progressively shallow. Often it isn't practical to stop down to a narrow aperture of f/16 or f/22 as the shutter speed will be too slow. Also, background detail becomes more defined and can prove distracting. Even in shooting situations where you are able to use a high f/number, depth-of-field may only be a matter of millimetres, making good technique and focusing essential.

More often than not you will want to record your subject in sharp focus throughout, from the head to the tip of its abdomen. Therefore, to maximise the depth-of-field available for any given f/number, carefully position your camera so its sensor plane is parallel with the subject. If you fail to do this, you risk the insect's body or wings drifting out of focus.

PARALLEL

NOT PARALLEL

> **"Bugs are highly sensitive to movement, as they are constantly trying to avoid predation"**

Without flash

With flash

Diffused flash

5 Using flash I'm not a big fan of flash and prefer to rely on natural light. That said, there are times when ambient or reflected light is just not sufficient and a supplementary burst of flash is essential. Normal flashguns can be used for shooting some macro subjects, but a ring- or twin-flash unit designed specifically for macro work is better suited. A ringflash is circular in design and attaches to the front of the lens, but as they're designed to illuminate the subject evenly, lighting can look flat and dull. A twin flash unit is more flexible and works using a similar principle, but consists of two individual heads that can be moved independently and their flash output varied to offer greater creative possibilities. However, they are expensive and only close-up enthusiasts will justify the added cost. A more realistic alternative is to simply use the camera's built-in flash. What integral units lack in flexibility, they make up for in convenience. While their position is fixed and they can't be used off-camera, they can be popped up whenever required. This is especially handy in situations where you have to work fast – like insect photography. They are most useful for adding a touch of fill-in. Just take care not to get too close as you risk the flash passing over the top of the subject. As a result, the built-in flash is best combined at reproduction ratios below 1:2 (half life-size). With the flash being so close, there is also the risk of fine detail and colour being washed out. Therefore, try softening with a flash diffuser or by taping tissue or greaseproof paper over the flash head.

Common insects
Here are five of the most likely insects you will find and photograph in the UK

Large red damselfly: There are many species of damselfly, but one of the most widespread is the large red. It's on the wing from May-August and favours ponds, lakes, streams and bogs

Garden spider: This arachnid is found in huge numbers in gardens, hedgerows, woodland clearings and meadows from July until mid-autumn. Its large web comprises radial and spiral threads

Red admiral butterfly: One of our most widespread butterflies. Easily enticed into gardens by planting nectar-rich plants like buddleia. Most commonly spotted during July and August

Four-spotted dragonfly: Has distinctive spots on the leading edge of each pair of wings. It flies from May-August and hunts along hedgerows and near wetland habitats

Angel shade moth: One of the more widespread moths, on the wing from May to October. Recognised by its forewing having a ragged margin and its pinkish triangular mark

Capturing colourful critters

Head outdoors to explore your garden for new ways that you can combine flowers and insects for striking results

Daniel Lezano: If you're lucky enough to have a garden, chances are you'll already be aware of its potential as a location for great nature photography. Flowers in full bloom provide a wonderful opportunity to capture some colourful and intricate close-ups, but have you ever considered compositions that deliberately combine plants and wildlife together? While sat in my garden, inspiration quite literally flew into view as a ladybird landed on some flowers in front of me, giving me the idea of combining a beautiful floral still-life with my garden visitor.

Get prepared for close-ups

Shooting close-ups is an extremely rewarding activity as you're able to discover, explore and capture an often overlooked miniature world. You'll need kit that's able to produce high-magnification images of small subjects within a short distance from your lens. The ideal option is a macro lens, which provides a life-size reproduction ratio (1:1) and a very close focusing distance, allowing you to fill the frame with small subjects. Use a tripod so that you can fine-tune the composition and leave your camera set up in position. It also means your images won't be ruined by shake if shutter speeds are slow. A small silver/white reflector is handy for filling in shadows, but isn't essential.

While it's possible that you may find a ladybird in the perfect position with the perfect backdrop, it's more likely that you'll need to find a suitable plant and backdrop, then introduce your ladybird into the scene.

Ladybirds are unlikely to hang around for long, so it's essential that you have everything ready before you place one on the plant. This is why a tripod is so important – you can set up the camera's position so the image frame is composed how you like it, prepare the camera settings and then, once you've introduced the

ladybird, you can start taking pictures. If the ladybird moves, try to coax it back into position rather than adjust the camera.

With close-ups, depth-of-field is limited even at high f/numbers, so make sure you've focused correctly. Select a single AF point rather than use multi-point AF, so you can be in control of exactly where the lens focuses. The central point is usually the most sensitive, but you can choose whichever AF point covers the corresponding area of the plant you want to focus on. If your camera allows you to select small groups of AF points, then use this option for added sensitivity. Start with an aperture setting between f/5 and f/8, then after a couple of frames, take a sequence at different aperture settings to capture images with the background slightly sharper or thrown further out of focus.

Once you've captured a set of images that you're happy with, make small adjustments to the camera angle and see how this affects the image. You may discover an angle that gives a better perspective of the flower or the ladybird, or one that gives a better background.

Ensure a perfect focus

While AF systems are excellent for everyday situations, they can struggle with macro, so you should be prepared to focus manually if required. If you stick to AF, you'll improve the chance of success if you switch from multi-point to single-point AF and select the AF point over your subject. Be ready to change AF points if your subject moves. If your DSLR allows you to select a small group of AF points, use it as it's ideal for this type of image. Finally, select continuous frame advance – by shooting a sequence you increase the chance of success.

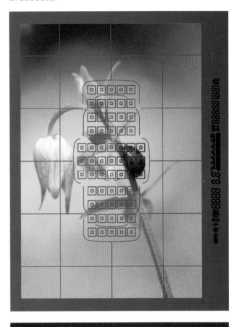

1 Get set up and ready With your camera tripod-mounted, position it so that you have the plant you want to use positioned neatly in the image frame. Ensure that it's well-lit and not obscured by other foliage. Take a test shot to ensure that the plant is focused correctly.

2 Introduce the ladybird Gently introduce the ladybird on to the plant. Whether it remains stationary or starts moving is out of your control, but you should ensure that the ladybird is in sharp focus and start firing the shutter immediately before it wanders off.

3 Make slight adjustments After taking a few frames, quickly review the images and make any changes you feel appropriate. Having reviewed the first set of pictures, I tilted the camera slightly so that the stem entered the frame at an angle to improve composition.

4 Fine-tune the image Don't be afraid to make more changes. I really liked the viewpoint but pulled back slightly to add contrast to the background. I also experimented more with aperture settings. This was taken at f/10, which added slightly more background detail.

Final image
Further tweaks gave this result,
with the ladybird and plant set
against a pleasing blurred
backdrop. Not bad for five
minutes' work in the garden!

Wild web wonders

See the beauty in dew-laden spiders' webs – shooting them up close is when you can truly appreciate the delicate details…

Ross Hoddinott: Rather than searching the web for ideas, why not get outside with your digital camera and search for a real web? Spiders spin beautiful cobwebs of sticky silk, and their constructions are intricate, often symmetrical and look stunning close up. Therefore, if you own a close-focusing zoom, close-up filter, extension tube or – better still – a dedicated macro lens, you will be able to capture stunning, frame-filling images.

Spiders live everywhere, so you shouldn't struggle to find a suitable web to photograph. They're easiest to find and look their most photogenic when smothered in tiny water droplets. Therefore, early morning after a clear, still night is the best time to look. Alternatively, you could spray one with water to create a similar effect by using a gardener's spray bottle to create a fine mist that won't damage the web. In autumn and winter, after a cold and frosty night, you might even find a frozen web, which is particularly photogenic and can make very arty, abstract-looking images by using a shallow depth-of-field, together with careful focusing. ➔

Handle with care!
Be careful not to knock the web or any grasses it might be joined to (it's easily done with a tripod leg). If you do, you may damage the web and knock the photogenic droplets to the ground

Final image
Using a black backdrop makes the water droplets sparkle beautifully. Just a few adjustments along the way to obtain pinpoint focusing and a shallow depth-of-field have transformed the result.

Essential kit

Reflector:
A compact, fold-away reflector is an essential close-up accessory. They are designed to bounce natural light onto miniature subjects in order to relieve ugly shadows. A reflector will normally create a more natural-looking form of illumination than flash. However, I have often employed a reflector (or its black cover) as a makeshift background for small subjects to create a simple backdrop. In some situations, you can even use a reflector's silver or white side in order to create high-key results.

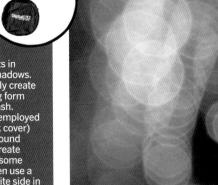

1 Take a test shot I don't have to search long before finding a dew-laden web. I compose the image quickly, including the entire web in the frame. I set an aperture of f/8, hoping that this will create sufficient depth-of-field to keep the web sharp, while not recording too much background detail. However, I don't pay enough attention to the background and the web doesn't stand out very well against the light backdrop.

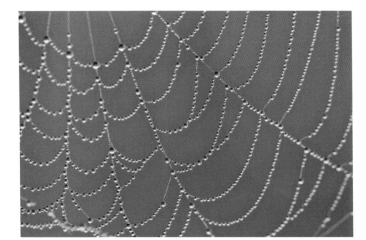

2 Alter viewpoint The subject's backdrop is often a major contributing factor to a photo's success or failure. By simply changing viewpoint, shooting angle, focal length or aperture, you can alter the background's colour and appearance. To eliminate the white sky from the image-space, I select a higher angle by extending the legs of my tripod. A grassy bank now creates a more attractive, green background. I also opt for a tighter composition.

3 Use a large aperture I want to create a more arty-looking result. So, I select a larger aperture of f/4, and place my set-up at an angle to the web. This will allow me to record just part of the web in focus. Focusing needs to be accurate when working with such a shallow depth-of-field. I check the image on the LCD monitor, zooming in to check the subject's sharpness. Unfortunately, my focusing isn't precise enough and the image is soft.

4 Ensure correct focus I try again. Using a shallow depth-of-field at this level of magnification allows the photographer to precisely direct the viewer's eye to a specific point of focus. If your camera has a preview button, use it to review the distribution of depth-of-field. This time I take an extra few moments to ensure my focusing is accurate and release the shutter remotely to prevent any camera movement spoiling the image.

5 Change backdrop Although happy with the previous shot, I feel a black backdrop will suit the subject better – thinking it would contrast starkly with the glistening water droplets. The cover of my reflector is black, so I hold it around 40cm behind the web and use the self-timer to trigger the shutter. Finally, I have the result I want. If you prefer a more colourful look, you could try using brightly coloured card to alter the appearance of the background.

How to shoot butterflies

Getting great shots of butterflies isn't as simple as point and shoot
– these nuggets of advice will help you achieve brilliant results...

Ross Hoddinott: The warmer, longer days of spring herald the emergence of a
whole host of spectacular insects. The skies buzz with bees and acrobatic
dragonflies, while among the undergrowth, colourful beetles and other mini
beasts busily scurry about. At first, photographing insects might hold limited
appeal, but in frame-filling close-up, their colour, beauty and intricate design is revealed.
Simply put, bugs make great pictures.

Of all the insects, butterflies are unquestionably the most popular and photogenic.
Thanks to their colourful and varied markings and graceful flight, most people adore them
– even self-confessed 'insect-phobes'. If you have attempted to photograph butterflies
before, maybe at a butterfly house or in your own back garden, you'll know that they can be
challenging subjects. They are easily disturbed, with a nasty habit of flying away just as you
are about to trigger the shutter. Even the largest UK species – like red admiral and peacock
– only have a wingspan of around 70mm, so to capture frame-filling images, a high level of
magnification is required. A macro lens is the perfect tool for the job – particularly one with
a focal length upwards of 90mm, as this provides a practical working distance. ➔

The perfect choice of optic is a macro lens – but as this is a costly item, it may make more sense to opt for an inexpensive close-up attachment instead, unless you are a dedicated close-up enthusiast. While cost-effective, the big drawback of using either a close-up filter or extension tubes is that you have to get closer to the subject, increasing the risk of frightening the flighty insects away. They do, however, provide a great introduction to the fascinating world of close-ups.

At the risk of stating the obvious, before you can photograph butterflies, you first need to locate them. Butterfly numbers are sadly in decline, so you may have to travel a few miles in order to find suitable environments. Different butterflies require different habitats and food plants – some enjoy grassland, while others prefer heathland, woodland or chalky downs. Research is the key. Spend time reading about butterfly types, where to find them and when. Search the internet for suitable local reserves, or better still, join your local Wildlife Trust and mix with the experts.

It is easiest to find butterflies during the day when they are most active. However, you will probably find they rarely settle or allow you close enough to take pictures. Instead, it is better to visit habitats early in the morning or during the evening when butterflies are less active or roosting among vegetation and tall grasses. Search carefully – always watching where you tread. Still days are best as even the slightest breeze will move the subject about and make it difficult to shoot.

Having located a butterfly, move yourself into position slowly. Avoid disturbing the surrounding vegetation or casting your shadow across the insect – doing so will frighten it away. On cool mornings, before it's warm enough for the insect to fly, it may be possible to use a tripod. This is hugely advantageous, aiding both pinpoint focusing and considered composition. If you have to shoot handheld, switch on the image stabiliser if you have it, or employ a workable fast shutter speed, upwards of 1/200sec, to eliminate camera movement. Before releasing the shutter, search the background for anything distracting. If necessary, adjust your shooting position to exclude anything that might draw the eye away from your subject.

Close-up attachments

You can quickly and cheaply transform your standard lens (or a short telephoto) into one capable of capturing great insect images by using a close-up attachment.

Auto extension tubes

These hollow rings fit between the camera and lens to reduce the minimum focusing distance without degrading image quality, although they do incur a degree of light loss. Auto extension tubes are compact, light and retain all the camera's functions. The most common lengths are 12mm, 20mm and 36mm – the wider the tube, the larger the reproduction ratio. For more information on auto extension tubes, see page 50.

Close-up filters

These screw onto the front of the lens and act like a magnifying glass. They are inexpensive, lightweight and available in varying filter diameters. They come in a range of strengths, typically +1, +2, +3 and +4 – the higher the number, the greater their magnification. They do not affect normal camera functions, but edge sharpness can suffer, and they are prone to 'ghosting', and spherical and chromatic aberration. Maximise image quality by selecting an aperture no smaller than f/8. For more information on close-up filters, see page 48.

Alternatively, select a wider aperture to help throw background detail quickly out of focus. Do bear in mind that at high magnifications depth-of-field is naturally shallow. Therefore, in order to keep the insect sharp throughout – and maximise the depth-of-field available at any given f/number – keep your camera parallel to the subject.

Admittedly, photographing butterflies can prove a fiddly and frustrating business. Be prepared to crawl through the undergrowth and put up with lots of 'near misses'. However, with good preparation and perseverance, you too will soon be taking great butterfly images.

Final image
A large aperture + tripod + reflector = a beautifully sharp shot of a butterfly with a shallow depth-of-field.

1 Locate the subject To photograph butterflies, you first need to know where, when and what to look for. For example, a local reserve close to me is home to hundreds of cuckoo flowers – a food plant of orange-tip butterflies. I set my alarm for daybreak and, after careful searching, find a butterfly clinging to one of the blooms.

2 Get into position I slowly move into picture-taking range, being careful not to disturb surrounding vegetation. A low viewpoint will often provide the most natural-looking results, so I lay on the ground and use my elbows as support. I select an aperture of f/16 to help generate a wide depth-of-field, but doing so creates a distracting, messy background.

3 Blurred background To help the butterfly stand out from the rest of the scene, I set a wide-ish aperture of f/5.6 to render the background as an attractive blur. The disadvantage of employing a lower f/number is that focusing has to be very precise due to the limited depth-of-field. To aid focusing, I carefully set up my tripod nearby and use LiveView.

4 Lighting Although the result is better, detail in the wing is obscured by shade. To relieve the shadows, I use a small reflector to angle light onto the butterfly and reveal the beautiful detail in its under-wing. In situations like this, when the subject is static, a reflector gives more control than using flash, and the final result still looks natural.

SIGMA

With a focal range that covers your everyday needs along with macro functionality, this large aperture, APS-C zoom lens combines superior performance with a conveniently compact form.

C Contemporary

17-70mm F2.8-4 DC MACRO OS HSM

Petal type lens hood included.

Available for Sigma, Canon, Nikon, Sony* and Pentax* AF cameras.

SIGMA **3**
3 YEAR UK WARRANTY
For registration and conditions log on to
www.sigma-imaging-uk.com/warranty

Compatible with APS-C digital SLRs only

*OS is not included in Sony and Pentax mounts

More on our new product line-up:

sigma-global.com

Sigma Imaging (UK) Ltd, 13 Little Mundells, Welwyn Garden City, Hertfordshire, AL7 1EW | Telephone: 01707 329 999 | Email: sales@sigma-imaging-uk.com | Website: www.sigma-imaging-uk.com

INDOOR TECHNIQUES

RAINY DAY? PAH! WHILE AWAY THE HOURS WITH FUN INDOOR TECHNIQUES...

SHOOT REFRACTIONS

CAPTURE PERFECT ROSES

TRY CROSS-POLARISATION

Strawberry splash

Shoot a summer-fruit splash that looks good enough to eat…

Jordan Butters: During summer, the nation is always gripped by tennis fever. And what says Wimbledon better than strawberries and cream – other than Cliff Richard, that is. Ideally, you want to be out shooting this step-by-step in the glorious sunshine, but if rain stops you playing, the game's not over. You can still create this summery image with lots of punch in your kitchen with the help of an off-camera flashgun and a colourful background. Summer fruit, vibrant colours and an action splash captured midair? If that doesn't whet your appetite for photography, then nothing will.

Set up

You'll need a space without any objects nearby so that you don't risk splashing them with liquid. To save time mopping up later, you should place paper towels down on any surface and use a tray or dish to catch the milk under the spoon.

Your spoon needs to be held in place securely so that it doesn't move out of focus when the strawberry lands. My home-brew solution comprises dining-room chairs, a selection of cookery books and a breadbin on top to weigh the spoon down and hold it steady. If you have a Wimberley Plamp, then this is ideal for positioning your props at the correct height. Set up the camera on a tripod, place the strawberry in the spoon, switch to manual focus and use LiveView with zoom to focus manually on the strawberry. You can use any colourful surface as a background, such as a large piece of coloured card, set a couple of feet away from the spoon and flash.

Exposure

Set your camera to manual mode and select your maximum flash sync speed, usually 1/160sec or 1/200sec, depending on your camera. Choose ISO 100 and connect your flashgun to the camera, either using a dedicated lead or wireless triggers, as I have. Set your flash to manual, select half-power and position your flashgun just above camera height and off to one side, pointing at the spoon. If you don't have a light stand to hand, you can always ask a volunteer to hold the flashgun for you. Choose a mid-aperture in order to capture enough of the splash in focus yet still render the background soft. I found f/7.1 worked for me. With the strawberry still in the spoon, fire a test shot. If it's underexposed, open the aperture or move the flashgun closer to the spoon; if it is overexposed, either close the aperture or move the flashgun further away. Finally, I position a reflector towards the back of my set-up to bounce some light on to the background to create a gradient.

Try different coloured backdrops or different fruit. Or even forgo the splash and pour on the cream from above for a mouthwatering summer image.

Pouring cream

Different background

■ **Composition:** Compose to allow space around the spoon for the splash to sit within the frame. The higher you drop the fruit, the higher the splash. It doesn't matter if some of the drops leave the frame, but you want to capture the majority of the splash.

■ **Liquid:** Different viscosity liquids create different splash effects; single cream was too thick and didn't form droplets, whereas fully skimmed milk was too translucent. I found that full-fat milk had just the right consistency for the splash that I wanted.

■ **Keep it clean:** Depending on your choice of focal length, your lens may be in the firing line of the splash, so fit a UV filter to the front of your lens to protect it. I had to check and clean the filter between shots to stop any milk spots spoiling the next shot.

Final image
Some tweaks were made using
Image>Adjustments>Curves to
boost contrast slightly and give
the final image plenty of punch.

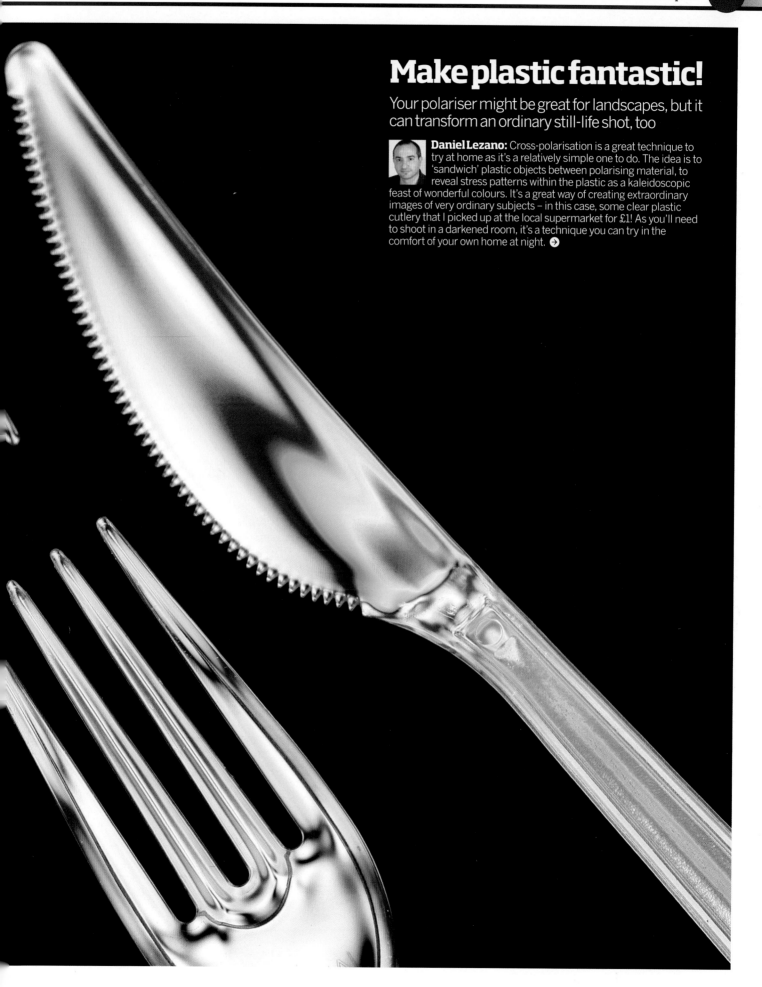

Make plastic fantastic!

Your polariser might be great for landscapes, but it can transform an ordinary still-life shot, too

Daniel Lezano: Cross-polarisation is a great technique to try at home as it's a relatively simple one to do. The idea is to 'sandwich' plastic objects between polarising material, to reveal stress patterns within the plastic as a kaleidoscopic feast of wonderful colours. It's a great way of creating extraordinary images of very ordinary subjects – in this case, some clear plastic cutlery that I picked up at the local supermarket for £1! As you'll need to shoot in a darkened room, it's a technique you can try in the comfort of your own home at night. ➔

Essential kit

Tripod, lightbox & cloth!

I used a macro lens to get in really close to small areas of my subject, but the tele-end of a standard zoom would be suitable, too. You'll need to use a tripod, as exposures will run into seconds, so a remote release is useful, too, though I used the self-timer and mirror lock-up facility of my Canon EOS 400D to minimise shake. A lightbox provides all the light you'll need and, apart from the polarisers, you're almost there. One extra bit of kit I'd recommend is a lens cloth and/or blower brush. Smears and dust will be obvious at such magnification! Use aperture-priority mode, start at f/8 for optimum sharpness, but feel free to change the aperture to vary depth-of-field. Multi-zone metering will work here, but apply exposure compensation if needed.

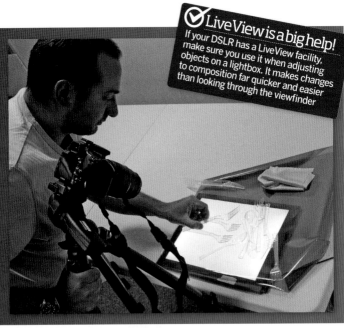

☑ **LiveView is a big help!**
If your DSLR has a LiveView facility, make sure you use it when adjusting objects on a lightbox. It makes changes to composition far quicker and easier than looking through the viewfinder

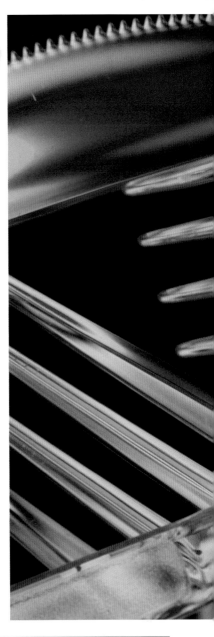

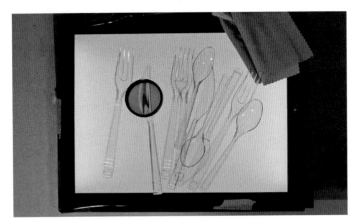

1 Choose your subject Cross-polarisation is all about revealing stress patterns in plastic, so colours will play a strong part in the success of the final image. However, equally important is the shape of the subject you choose, which will add extra interest to the composition. Choosing subjects with defined outlines really works – for this step-by-step, I decided to shoot a cutlery set.

Technique watch!

Cross-polarisation

This technique involves placing a plastic subject between two polarisers. The easiest way to do this is to have a circular polarising filter attached to your lens and then have another polariser resting on a lightbox, with the plastic object(s) on top. You can use another screw-in polarising filter on the lightbox, but it limits the size of the subject you can use. A better alternative is to buy a sheet of polarising gel, which covers the whole lightbox surface. They're a little pricy in the UK, but our readers have told us of an internet firm in the Far East (www.3dlens.com) that offers a good quality, affordable option.

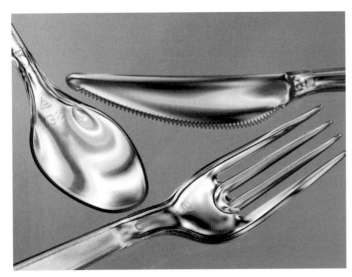

2 Adjust your set-up as you go It's worth jotting down a list of set-ups before you start and add to it as you go along – as you'll discover, once you start, you'll be changing the arrangement of objects, zooming in and out (or raising the tripod up and down) as you think up new angles to try. Start off with a simple composition like this and be more creative as you get the hang of things.

3 Rotate your polariser Once you've set up the composition, look through the viewfinder (or better still use LiveView) and rotate the ring of the circular polarising filter. As if by magic, you'll see the background change from white to black and colours transform your plastic subjects. Stop turning the ring once you've a solid black background and the most intense colours, and shoot away!

Final image
The image on the opening spread is my favourite, but this one runs it a close second. The whole shoot only took 30 minutes to set up and shoot and I managed several images I'm happy with. Do it yourself and I'm sure you'll have similar success.

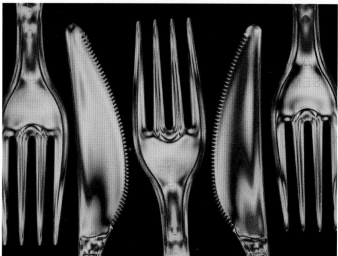

4 Try out different compositions As I went through my list of shots, I started to concentrate more on the fork and the knife, as their shapes made them far more photogenic than the spoon. As well as shooting from directly above the lightbox, I then tried lowering the tripod and shooting from an angle. I also tried using a wide aperture to reduce depth-of-field to vary my effects.

5 Clean as you go Despite trying to keep the cutlery as clean as possible, there was no way of preventing dust and fluff floating through the air from settling on it. It's worth doing a quick clean every couple of minutes as it's a far quicker option than having to remove dust and debris in Photoshop. The problem is accentuated when you start shooting macro close-ups such as this.

Capture the beauty of a rose

Close-ups of flowers require attention to detail to capture their true beauty – follow our guide for a blooming lovely still-life…

Daniel Lezano: If you've never tried photographing a flower, I'd suggest you give it a go. As a photographer who concentrated mainly on portraiture, the enjoyment I found from composing my first ever flower still-life came as nothing short of a revelation. It's an incredibly rewarding form of photography, which allows you to practise your skills with composition and lighting, as well as testing your creativity by trying to find different angles and viewpoints to shoot from. The sheer variety of beautiful flowers available will give you endless options for your still-life. My personal favourite is the gerbera, but it's run a close second by the elegant beauty of the rose. However, I find the gerbera to be a far easier flower to photograph, as its shape allows you to capture it from all sorts of angles and crops. In my view, the rose is a much harder proposition; it is more fragile and the folds of its petals can mean that not every one you find is a suitable subject for photography. In the past, when I've bought roses, I've specifically headed to a good florist and delved through their selection for the perfect subject. For this step-by-step, however, I snipped roses from a neighbour's garden (with permission, of course!), to show that it is possible to find a suitable subject even among ordinary flowers from the garden. ➔

The set-up: The great thing about close-up flower photography is you don't need an elaborate set-up. The area close to the French doors in my dining room provides all the light I need for this shoot. The rose is balanced in a half-filled plastic water bottle to hold it in position, while my DSLR with macro lens is set up on a tripod.

I find that shooting a flower indoors offers two key advantages: wind blowing the flower isn't an issue and shooting in the shade provides a far gentler light. Finally, it's worth keeping a silver reflector on hand should you need to bounce some light back into the scene.

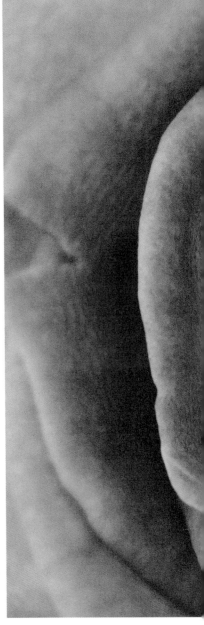

Essential kit

Macro lens and tripod

Because we're trying to fill the frame with a very small subject, a macro lens is pretty much an essential bit of kit. It will allow you to focus within a few centimetres from your subject and exclude the background from the frame, so that the entire image is filled with your flower. Now it's fair to say that you can get away with shooting handheld here, especially if your camera or lens has an image stabilisation facility, but I'd highly recommend that you do use a tripod. Using one will allow you to fine-tune your compositions, ensure your focusing is absolutely precise (this is absolutely critical with macro photography) and also let you shoot a series of identical shots at different aperture settings so that you can later choose the one that you prefer.

1 Achieve correct focus I set aperture-priority mode and, for optimum quality, a low ISO of 100. One thing I haven't set yet is the autofocus. I leave it at multi-point, just to demonstrate what happens. With all AF points active, the camera focuses on the closest part of the subject, which is on the far right of the frame. Switching to single-point AF and setting the AF point over the area I want to focus sorts this out. Another option is to use manual focus.

2 Fine-tune the composition With focusing solved, take a shot and check the histogram – you should find that unless the flower is very light or dark, your exposures are correct. Now concentrate on the composition. Make small adjustments to the tripod head, raise or lower the legs and move the flower until you're happy with how it's framed. LiveView proves very useful, as you can monitor changes more easily than if using the viewfinder.

Final image
The advantage of buying from a florist is that your subject will have fewer imperfections. This garden rose had a few discoloured areas, but they were easily cleaned up with the Healing Brush Tool in Photoshop. After 15 minutes of photography and five minutes of Photoshop, I've a beautiful still-life of a flower to add to my colourful collection!

3 Use a reflector I am pleased with the composition of the image, but not so happy that the side of the flower closest to the window is much brighter than the right side. I balance this out by resting my reflector on the tripod leg closest to the flower. The light it bounces back is subtle, but I'm happy with the difference it makes to the image.

4 Set the aperture Once you're happy with the composition and lighting, take a series of exposures at one-stop intervals from maximum to minimum aperture to give you a complete set, from minimal depth-of-field to as much as possible in focus. To minimise shake in the longer exposures, use the self-timer or a remote release to fire the shutter.

Look at fruit salad with fresh eyes!

Backlighting fruit is a classic technique, but the trick is to get your composition right. Here's how it's done…

Ross Hoddinott: Our homes are full of potential pictures, you just need to look at everyday objects with a fresh, creative eye. Small objects are the easiest to illuminate creatively, allowing you plenty of control over the type of lighting – natural or artificial – and also its direction. One of my favourite forms of light is backlighting. Translucent subjects, like coloured plastics, glass and leaves look particularly attractive and eye-catching when backlit. The easiest way to create this type of lighting indoors is to use a lightbox. Many digital converts will already have one from their days of viewing slides. However, if you don't own one, they are relatively cheap to buy or make. All you have to do now is find a suitable subject to shoot. Food is a particularly good still-life subject, especially fruit, with its bright colours and variety of textures. I was making the family a fruit salad one evening when inspiration struck.

1 Prepare your subject I return from the local grocers with an assortment of fruit including apples, pears, an orange, a lemon and a lime, grapes and a pomegranate. I want to highlight their shape and form, so I carefully cut each one into thin slices to create a photogenic, translucent cross-section of each fruit, ready to arrange on my lightbox.

Technique watch!

Optimise depth-of-field: When you're taking close-ups from overhead, optimise depth-of-field by keeping the camera's sensor – that sits parallel to the rear LCD panel – square to the subject. By doing so, you will keep all objects of similar height in focus. If the camera is at an angle to the subject, areas of it will drift out of focus, spoiling the crisp, fresh look of the fruit and lessening the impact of the shot.

Essential kit

Lightbox: Backlighting small translucent objects indoors is easy with the help of a lightbox. They are available in a variety of sizes, but A4 size or larger is probably the most versatile and useful. The lightbox can be placed on a tabletop or on the floor, then, with the help of a tripod, position your camera overhead. A lightbox can also create striking silhouettes of small, solid objects.

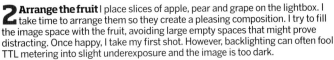

2 Arrange the fruit I place slices of apple, pear and grape on the lightbox. I take time to arrange them so they create a pleasing composition. I try to fill the image space with the fruit, avoiding large empty spaces that might prove distracting. Once happy, I take my first shot. However, backlighting can often fool TTL metering into slight underexposure and the image is too dark.

3 Adjust exposure I check the histogram, which confirms the photo is underexposed, so I apply positive (+) exposure compensation of 2/3EV. This remedies the problem and the subsequent image is exposed correctly. However, it lacks colour and impact. This type of shot evolves as you go along. Experimentation is the key, so I decide to try some different fruits.

4 Try different subjects In order to add some much-needed colour, I switch to citrus fruits, using a slice each of orange, lemon and lime. I like the contrasting colours and sizes of the fruit. I arrange them so that their edges meet and the backlighting really emphasises their form and transparency. However, the white gaps between the fruit are distracting and don't make the best composition, so I decide I need to fill the entire frame with colour.

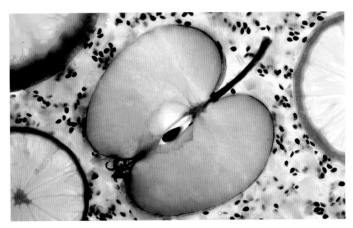

5 Introduce a focal point I scoop out the insides of some kiwi fruit and then carefully place the pulp around my fruit slices. I decide to make a slice of apple my key focal point, as this has the most interesting and recognisable outline. I use the slices of citrus fruit to balance the composition. However, I feel I need to add a splash of red for extra punch to contrast with the greens and yellows that dominate the image.

Final image

I carefully remove the bright red seeds of a pomegranate and use them to replace the kiwi fruit. This adds the colour contrast and impact the previous shots had lacked. A vertical composition works best. The result – a simple but striking still-life taken in the comfort of indoors. And, the leftover fruit made for a delicious fruit salad!

Alphabet soup

Raid your kitchen cupboard – it spells fun for you and your camera…

Ross Hoddinott: I possess a complete lack of culinary skills… just ask my poor wife! I'm hopeless in the kitchen, which is why it is safer for everyone concerned if I photograph food rather than prepare it for eating! Opening a tin of beans or soup is just about my limit. My little girls love alphabet soup and it was watching my older daughter making words with the letters that got me thinking about the picture potential. I decided to raid the cupboard and have fun spelling out specific words using the alphabet soup. This is a fun shot to try and it couldn't be easier or cheaper to do. You can buy a couple of small tins for under a pound at your local supermarket, and then all that is required are a few everyday household bits and pieces. I used a small still-life table to arrange my set-up, although a simple tabletop set-up in your kitchen or living room would do the job equally well. Rather than using flash, the soft natural light from an adjacent window is ideally suited to this type of still-life image. Time to start spelling…

Getting started:
I used a white products table as my base, but any table or kitchen surface will work well. Keep some kitchen towel nearby too: alphabet soup is messy stuff and easy to get on your hands when you are picking out and arranging your letters with tweezers. You don't want to transfer tomato sauce from your hand to your valuable camera gear!

1 Choose your letters Firstly, I opened the tin of soup and poured the contents into a flat, white dish. Using tweezers, I began picking out the letters I required. In this instance, I chose to spell out PHOTO DIY. However, even with tweezers, you have to be gentle not to damage or break the letters, but after a few minutes, I soon found the letters I needed for my chosen phrase.

2 Take a test shot I thought it would be fun to have my words on a spoon as it would help the letters stand out and the spoon would add visual interest. Again using tweezers, I arranged the letters. However, while the idea was good, in practice the letters all slid together as the metal is scooped, distorting their shape and making the words tricky to read.

3 Try something new Carefully, I moved the letters back onto the dish. To ensure PHOTO DIY stood out, I left a small gap around the words. I then held the spoon in position, just above the dish, using a clamp. I focused on the spoon, but to ensure the words in the background were still distinguishable, I selected an aperture of f/11 to provide sufficient depth-of-field.

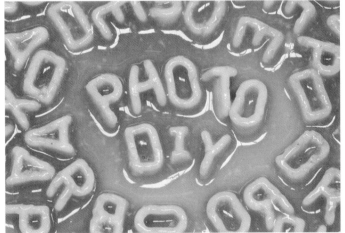

4 Crop in tight I wasn't happy with either of my previous efforts, so I decided to dispense with the spoon – instead of creating interest, it was proving a distraction. This time, I cropped in tighter, filling the frame with the alphabet soup. The window light provided ample lighting and I used a tripod to ensure my picture remained shake-free at an exposure of 1/4sec at f/11.

Final image
I decided the alphabet soup would look better shot in a vertical composition. The format change meant I had to rearrange the surrounding letters, leaving a larger gap around PHOTO DIY.

I AM A THRILL-SEEKER

I AM THE NIKON D7100. I am photography unlimited. Offering breathtaking images thanks to the precision of a 24.1 MP resolution and the professional level 51-point autofocus system. With an additional 1.3x crop mode for extra telephoto effect, I expand DX possibilities. All combined in an extremely durable, weatherproof and portable body for great performance, wherever you go, whatever you do. I am for the ones who go further. **www.nikon.co.uk**

At the heart of the image

Splash out for the perfect shot!

Take a bow, splash crowns – use milk for a whole new take on high-speed water-droplet shots

Andreas Stridsberg: While capturing water droplets may not be a new technique, fans of it should be intrigued to hear of a different way to approach this type of high-speed photography. Using the same equipment and theory for capturing water droplets, you can also create abstract shapes called splash crowns.

While for water droplets you can get away with a thin liquid, to achieve splash crowns, the fluid has to have a thicker viscosity, like whole-fat milk, for example. This higher viscosity results in very intricate shapes being formed when a droplet falls from a height and impacts on the liquid's surface. You can make these splash crowns look even more creative by adding food colourings to the milk for a technicolour effect.

In essence, this isn't technically difficult, but it does demand a high level of patience as your timing – to release the shutter just as the milk droplet hits the surface – has to be spot-on. However, don't get too frustrated if you can't get results within a few frames as you'll be sure to crack it before too long.

Macro magic

Dedicated macro lenses are perfect for this type of shot as they have a life-size (1:1) reproduction ratio, so the object appears as wide on the sensor as it is in real life, resulting in frame-filling shots. However, if you don't have a macro lens, consider buying a set of close-up filters or extend your zoom to its maximum focal length and move in as close as you can, stopping when the lens can no longer focus.

1 Set up With my DSLR secured on a tripod and in position, I place my stand and clamp on a clean black table with a dark sheet as the background. Next, I pour some whole-fat milk into a glass, ready to use as my viscous liquid.

2 Set the flash I position my flashgun side-on, around 10-20cm away from the splash zone, setting the unit to manual mode and adjusting its power to 1/64. The flash needs to trigger while off-camera, so use a corded or wireless trigger.

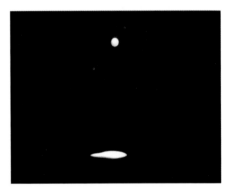

3 Create a puddle Using the syringe, I create a small puddle of milk on the glass-topped table. This will give my lens something to focus on and also help create a splash later. If your lens is struggling, place a pencil in the milk puddle, establish focus and then switch to manual focus.

4 Dial in camera settings You'll need to adjust your settings depending on how much light is in the room, but a good starting point is 1/125sec at f/8. I also stick with a low ISO rating of 200, but again, you may want to adjust this depending on your set-up.

5 Take a test shot Here's the tricky part. With your remote release in the one hand and the syringe fixed in its clamp (around 30cm above your surface), release a drop of milk and fire the shutter as it lands on the milk puddle you placed in step three. I triggered this shot too early.

6 Get your timing right With a bit of patience, you'll soon get the hang of it. To maximise your chances, increase your target by adding more milk to the table. After three or four attempts, I finally get it right.

7 Add interest To bring more colour to the shot, I dry my table and then position coloured card under a sheet of glass. I then reapply the milk drop and also add some food colouring. The results are quite dynamic.

Final image
The great thing about this technique
is that no two shots will be the same.
Experiment with different card and
food colourings to see how creative
you can make your splash crowns.

Shoot some smoke trails

Create smoke trails with a difference – adding colour in Photoshop for a twist…

Sailesh Patel: An easy way to create stunning, abstract images with a mystical air is to shoot some smoke trails. I've used incense sticks for this technique as they are relatively safe for indoor use and provide just the right viscosity of smoke for this sort of result. As the smoke always rises in a slightly different way, there's an infinite variety of shapes and patterns to shoot.

Once you've captured your smoke-trail shots, there's also a wealth of options for adjusting them to create some truly magical results. Each trail can be coloured, flipped, dodged, burned or distorted in post-production to create other shapes. There is literally no limit to the potential of this technique. However, it is important to ensure that the incense sticks are used responsibly, as they can cause fires. Make sure that once they are lit, you stay with them at all times for safety reasons.

1 Set up I cover a studio table with a black cloth, adding a sheet of glass (a ceramic dish will also suffice) to reduce any risk of fire. I then stick the incense stick to the glass with Blu-Tack. I mount my flashgun behind the incense, with a piece of black card stuck to the far side of it, to prevent the light spilling out onto the background. I set up my camera (and wireless flash trigger) on a tripod, and open windows to ensure that the room is properly ventilated.

2 Dial in settings I set my camera to manual mode and switch the lens to manual focus, prefocusing for the area just above the incense. I set a shutter speed of 1/200sec – my camera's fastest flash sync speed – and an aperture of f/14, to give me sufficient depth-of-field. I also set my camera to record the images in Raw format, as this will not only provide the best quality images possible, it will also allow me to enrich the blacks in the conversion process within Photoshop later.

3 Shoot the incense Once I'm ready to start shooting, I carefully light the incense, making sure that the stick is stuck securely and in no danger of falling onto the black fabric. For comfort's sake, I use a remote release to fire the shutter. Once I have taken between 30 and 40 shots, I make sure that the incense is completely extinguished and then review the images on my LCD screen. I'm mainly looking to check that no light from the flashgun has hit the background.

Original | Inverted

4 Post-process Once I am satisfied with the results, I upload the images to my computer. In Adobe's Camera Raw converter, I use the Blacks slider to darken the background before opening the file. I then use the Eraser tool in Photoshop to clean up any unwanted smoke spread. Next, I invert the image (*Image>Adjustments>Invert*). This will change the smoke trails to a hazy black and the background to a crisp, pure white – making the image stand out more.

5 Add colour To add further interest to the shot and give it real impact, I decide to add some colour. In Photoshop's Hue/Saturation palette, I tick the *Colorize* and *Preview* boxes, before moving the sliders around until I'm happy. I choose this rich red colour, and a saturation of 75 per cent. I then save the image under a new file name. Next, I open a different image and repeat steps four and five, but I decide to colour the second smoke trail with a rich blue.

6 Merge images With both shots open, I copy the blue one (*Select>Select All; Edit>Copy*) and paste it onto the red image (*Edit>Paste*). I reduce the Opacity of the blue image and move it around until it looks good. To align the images, I use the *Free Transform* tool (*Ctrl+T*). I then return the Opacity of the blue layer to 100% and change the Layer Blending Mode from Normal to *Multiply*. Finally, I flatten the image (*Layer>Flatten Image*) and save as a new file.

Final image

After a few final tweaks to the Curves, Saturation and Contrast, I'm very happy with my final image. It is a very colourful abstract that could look great as a canvas print on any wall.

Fun with refraction

Combining water droplets and sweets can create dynamic and colourful shots

Ross Hoddinott: Refraction is the directional shift or 'bending' of light rays as they leave one density and enter another – it is the reason your legs look shorter underwater when viewed from above the surface. The way in which water refracts and reflects its surroundings, and nearby objects, offers endless creative potential for photographers. Water droplets act like tiny 'lenses' reflecting perfect, miniature, reversed images within them. Photographed in close-up, you can capture this striking effect. Colourful flowers look particularly good when photographed through a water droplet – creating an 'image within an image'. You could try taking pictures outside after rainfall or a dewy night when foliage is dripping. However, this gives you little control over the image reflected within your droplet, and you also have to consider wind movement. Instead, why not arrange a simple tabletop set-up indoors and create your own refraction photos? You can have all sorts of fun using different subjects: for example, you could use text, flowers, a flag, a clock or even food. With just the aid of a few household bits and bobs, I decided to create my own water droplet images...

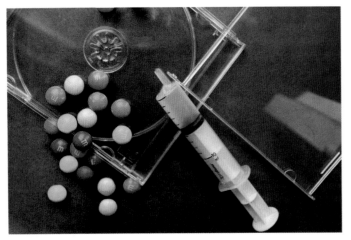

1 Choose your subject I want to create a fun, colourful image. So after much deliberating, I decide to photograph the refracted image of some colourful sweets. To do so, I need some glass or clear plastic to place my droplets on – I opt for the lid of a CD case. To create and position my reflective droplets, I decide to use a syringe, but a dropper or water spray would also work.

Essential kit

Tripod & remote release
To achieve enough depth-of-field to keep both the droplet and refracted image in acceptable focus, you will need to select a small aperture. This will result in a slow shutter speed, making the use of a tripod essential to keep the camera shake-free and to allow you to accurately select your point of focus. Capturing frame-filling images of tiny water droplets requires shooting at a relatively high level of magnification – when even the tiniest movement seems greatly exaggerated. Using a remote release is preferable to physically releasing the shutter with your finger, which can create slight vibrations that can soften the final image. If you don't have a remote release, use your camera's self-timer facility.

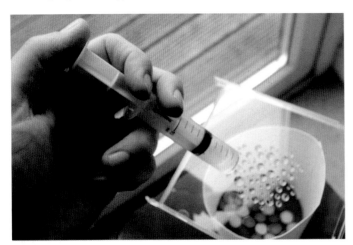

2 Create droplets I arrange the sweets on a black surface. I then roll up and tape a sheet of white card into a cylindrical shape, placing it around the sweets, to help reflect light evenly and to create a makeshift 'stand' on which to place the CD lid. Using the syringe, I carefully create a series of tiny droplets on the CD case – each drop creating a refracted image of the sweets below.

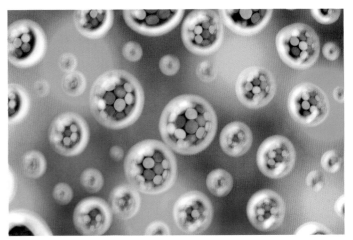

3 Compose your shot Using a tripod, I position my camera directly overhead, keeping it parallel to maximise depth-of-field. I compose my shot and carefully focus on the refracted image within the droplets – not the droplets' surfaces. I start with a large aperture of f/4, but the depth-of-field is too shallow and everything other than the refracted images is out of focus.

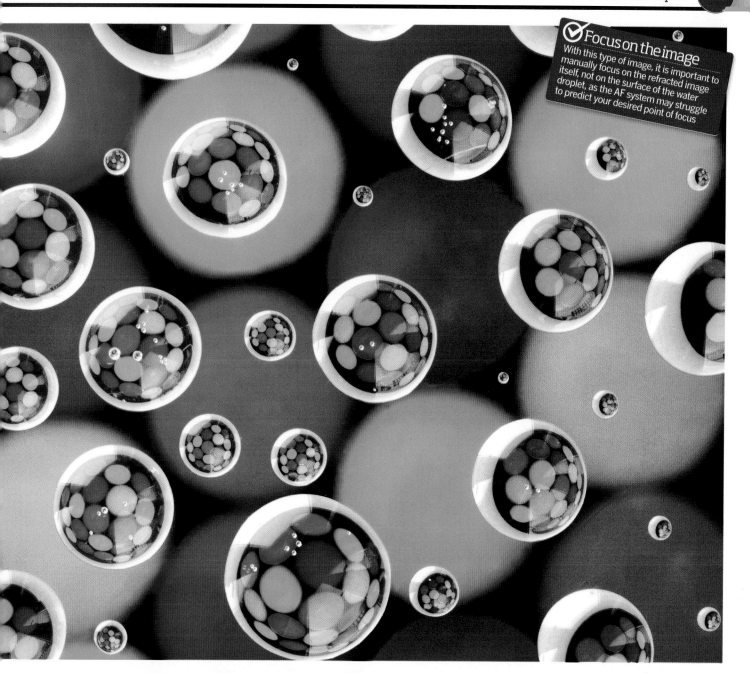

Focus on the image
With this type of image, it is important to manually focus on the refracted image itself, not on the surface of the water droplet, as the AF system may struggle to predict your desired point of focus

4 Take a test shot I change the aperture to f/22 to increase depth-of-field. The resulting shutter speed is two seconds, so a tripod and remote release proves essential. The result has far more impact – the droplets are in focus, and the sweets behind make a colourful background. However, dust and scratches on the plastic are also now visible because of the smaller aperture.

5 Clean up your image Even though I had wiped over the plastic case before I began shooting, tiny marks are obvious across the image. Using a combination of Photoshop's Clone Tool and Healing Brush, I carefully clean the image. I then adjust the Levels to increase contrast, upping the saturation slightly, too, in Hue/Saturation, to add impact.

A macro marvel

Water droplets are particularly effective when they're photographed on flowers. Our step-by-step shows you how

Luoana Negut: When it comes to taking great macro photographs, composition and focusing are critical. The smallest detail can make or break a picture, so when trying this photo project, make sure you're equipped with your eye for detail and loads of patience. Including droplets in your flower pictures adds the interest factor to a standard still-life shot. Contrary to popular belief, water isn't the best medium to use for this technique as it's difficult to control and the slightest movement can cause the droplet to spread. Saline solution (available from an optician), or a clear liquid that's thicker than water, keeps its droplet form better (see over the page for more info). While you could try practically any flower, gerberas are an ideal choice for this technique as their flat petals make it easier for the droplet to stay still.

Once you've mastered balancing the droplet on a petal, you need to be aware of how the light reflects and refracts in the water and position the camera, or flower, so it's not too distracting. A macro lens with at least a 1:2 (half life-size) reproduction ratio, or even better 1:1 (life-size), and a short focusing distance works well. I used a 60mm, but a 100mm would be even easier because you won't have to work so close to the flower to get frame-filling shots. Using a black background can yield some striking results as it keeps the focus on the brightly coloured flower, but you could use any complementary colour to your flower to give your shots a different look. There is a lot of experimentation involved in this technique, but when you get it right, it can result in some striking still-lifes. ➔

H₂O just won't do

Water is too thin to use for this technique; as soon as you drop it on a petal it quickly changes form and it's difficult to get a perfect sphere. You need a liquid that's thicker and can hold its droplet form; sugared water is okay, but saline solution for contact lenses, as used here, is ideal.

Set-up: Using window light is one of the easiest ways to try this technique. Luckily, it's a cloudy day so the light is really diffused, but I have a reflector at the ready in case the light gets a bit stronger and I need to fill in some shadows. Lining part of the window with black card provides the dark background, but make sure you position the flower so it's well illuminated. Here I raised it a little and placed it about 15cm away from the background.

Final image
Getting the centre of the flower in the picture adds context and the shallow depth-of-field places extra emphasis on the droplet.

1 **Focus on a droplet** Use a syringe or eyedropper to carefully place a droplet on the tip of a petal. If you do it in the middle it can get lost among the petals. Set aperture-priority mode and single-point AF, and get as close as you can to the droplet for a frame-filling shot. As there is a very shallow depth-of-field with close-ups, and the droplet curves away from the camera, you may need a mid-aperture like f/6.3 just to get the droplet in focus.

2 **Correct exposure** By using a black background, your camera may compensate for the dark tones by overexposing the shot. Correct it by dialling in one or two stops of negative exposure compensation.

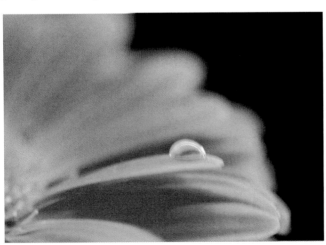

3 **Get perfect focus** Make sure the point of focus is on the water droplet to render it pin-sharp. If the lens struggles to focus, you may be too close to the flower or there may not be enough contrast. If it's the latter, switch to manual focus. If your shutter speed is slower than 1/30sec, you may find pressing the shutter causes shake. Minimise this risk by using the mirror lock-up facility if available, as well as the self-timer or a remote release.

4 **Look for the best highlights** As water refracts and reflects light, you may find that the droplet adopts some distracting highlights. Ideally, the highlight should run along the top edge of the droplet with minimal reflections. By backing the droplet against the flower, you should get a refracted image of the flower, or at least its colour, in the droplet. Experiment with the positioning of the flower and your camera angle.

5 Try different compositions The smallest change to your angle or framing can make a dramatic difference to the impact of a macro shot. Try different viewpoints, petals and angles to get the best composition: you may want to skew the camera to get more in the frame. Including some of the gerbera's centre in the picture can give context, or try a very shallow depth-of-field to blur the petals for an extreme close-up.

6 Add interest Try putting more than one droplet on a petal for more interesting results. It's tricky, but the best pictures are when the droplets are relatively the same size. You could try using a wide aperture and focusing on one of the droplets or use a narrower aperture to get all the beads in focus. The more direct the lighting, the darker the shadows may be, so be ready with a reflector or a piece of white card to fill them in.

How to use focus stacking to extend depth-of-field

The biggest challenge with macro photography is getting sufficient depth-of-field. The solution: focus stacking. Here we show you how…

Caroline Wilkinson: The longer the lens, the closer the subject-to-camera distance, and the wider the aperture, the shallower the depth-of-field. All these factors come into play with macro photography, which is why achieving front-to-back focus is often impossible. While using your lens's minimum aperture can help, it isn't always enough and what depth-of-field it does provide is at the expense of some softening from diffraction and extended exposure times.

Focus stacking is a way around this: the process consists of taking several images focusing on different focal planes, then combining them for maximum depth-of-field. It's quite a complicated technique to master, but it's easier if you do the in-camera work well and methodically. There are automated programs that can stack images for you, but we've found the results aren't as accurate as when you take control and process the stack yourself in Photoshop or Lightroom.

It's important the subject and camera don't move between shots, which is why static subjects are often best to practise on. For optimum sharpness, we suggest using an aperture of f/8-f/11, depending on the light

levels. If you need a faster shutter speed, consider using flash or opening up the aperture, but be aware that a wider aperture will mean you need to take more pictures to maximise depth-of-field, resulting in a more complicated stack. For this step-by-step, we used f/11. Take the pictures in a logical order – for instance, bottom to top – to make it easier when you open and order the files in Photoshop.

Depth-of-field: Four images, taken at f/11 and focused at different points, make up the final image

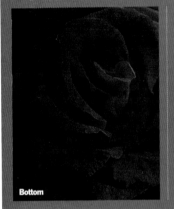

Bottom

Middle

Top third

Back petals

Finishing in Photoshop

1 Open the images Once they're open, select a picture as your base image (in this case, it's the one with the bottom part of the frame in focus). Use the **Move Tool** to then click and drag the other layers, preferably in order of focal planes, on top of your base image. You'll see that each image creates a layer in the Layers palette. You may find it helps to name the layers, too.

2 Sort out files The fewer files you have to work with, the easier the process will be, so take a moment to flick the eye icons next to each layer on and off to decide if every layer you're going to stack has a fundamental part of making the image sharp. Look at the images very carefully as, depending on the aperture you used, the depth-of-field might be very shallow.

3 Align images When you focus on different areas of an image, the perspective can change slightly, meaning not every image fills the frame the same way and layers may not line up perfectly on top of one another. To get around this, select each layer in the Layers palette by holding down **Shift** and clicking on **Edit>Auto Align** and wait for Photoshop to finish processing.

4 Use Layer Masks The next step hinges on your eye for detail and practice. Apply a Layer Mask to all your layers using the **Add Layer Mask** icon at the bottom of the Layers palette. Then use the **Brush Tool** loaded with **Black** paint to 'paint' over the Layer Masks and hide the areas that are out of focus. If you make a mistake, switch to **White** paint to reveal the area.

5 Final edits Once you've completed the stack, you may want to make tonal or sharpening adjustments. Select all the layers again and press **ctrl+alt+shift+E** (**cmd+alt+shift+E** on Mac) to create a combined layer. To boost contrast, duplicate this layer, set a **Soft Light** Blend Mode and reduce **Opacity** until you're happy. You can also apply a **Levels** adjustment layer.

Final image:

If your image needs some sharpening, duplicate the combined layer again and go to *Filter>Sharpen>Unsharpen Mask* and adjust the slider to suit. You should now be left with a still-life that's sufficiently crisp front to back.

Shoot a romantic still-life

A ring and a book are brilliant subjects to play with shadows and create a beautifully simple, but emotive, still-life. Read on to discover how to do it…

Caroline Wilkinson: A shot like this is very popular with wedding photographers and it's no surprise considering how quick and easy it is to do. All you need is one light source placed behind the ring, such as a desk lamp, torch or flashgun, so that when combined with the folds of a page, it creates a heart-shaped shadow. Although for this image I used my wedding ring, why not try using a red, circular filter to cast a larger red heart or a close-up filter to magnify the word 'Love' on the page? Having tried the technique with both a standard lens and a macro lens, the best results came from having the 1:5 reproduction ratio combined with a beautiful shallow depth-of-field to isolate the focal point. A standard zoom will work, too, but you won't be able to get as close to the ring as with a macro lens and depth-of-field may extend further. It's a perfect shot for a pending anniversary or recent engagement – not that you need a reason to try out this sentimental still-life.

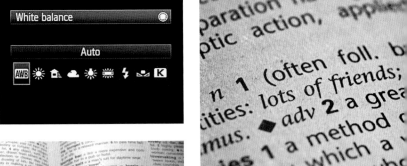

White Balance

If you're shooting in JPEG or TIFF you'll need to select the correct White Balance (colour temperature) preset for your lighting set-up. For instance, as I'm using a tungsten desk lamp I would have selected the tungsten preset or risk the camera getting it wrong with Auto WB if I'm using mixed lighting, such as a touch of daylight and tungsten. As it was shot in Raw, I could correct the White Balance in Photoshop's Raw conversion software. For a complete guide to Raw, see the March and April 2013 issues of *Digital SLR Photography* magazine.

1 Set up A soft-backed book will be easier to manage for this technique, as you'll need to keep the open book as flat as possible to be able to balance the ring. Don't break the spine to keep the pages flat, instead secure them with a weight or Blu-Tack if you have to. I position the desk lamp behind the book and at a 45° angle, as it seems to cast the strongest shadow.

2 Play around with composition Unless you want to secure the ring using Blu-Tack, which can be unsightly, you'll need to find a ring that is wide enough to balance on its own. But even if your ring can't stand up on its side you can still create an attractive heart-shaped shadow by playing with the angle of the light. For this DIY, though, I decide to change the ring to one with a thicker band.

3 Adjust the lighting The strength, shape and length of the shadow will depend on the angle and distance between the lamp and the book. The closer and lower the light is to the ring, the shorter and stronger the shadow will be. Remember to turn off all other lights in the room, too. I set the camera to aperture-priority mode and select an aperture of f/10 to begin with.

4 Achieving correct depth-of-field After a few tries it becomes clear that the best shots use a wide aperture with the lens close to the ring. The trick is in finding the right f/stop to get sufficient depth-of-field for the ring, but blur any distracting words. I also play with the focal point, switching between the word 'Love' and the ring to see which has the most impact when in focus.

Final image
To get this antique look, I use Photoshop to tweak the Color Balance and use the Burn Tool to darken the edges with a soft brush.

5 **Ensure sharp results** With one light source and the lens close to the book, light levels are low, resulting in slow shutter speeds. A large aperture also means the plane of focus is shallow, so although I am using a tripod, getting the shot sharp is challenging. You may find that simply pressing the shutter button will create enough shake to blur a shot, so you may want to use a remote release.

6 **Experiment with viewpoints** Remember to try out different compositions and viewpoints, such as taking a bird's-eye or eye-level approach. Don't just play it safe by keeping the book and ring central in the frame; use the rule-of-thirds and diagonal lines to make the picture instantly stronger. I try various compositions until I find my final preferred image.

Love the bokeh

Low-light photography opens up so many possibilities for brilliant bokeh shots. This technique is close to our heart…

Caroline Wilkinson: Shallow depth-of-field is one of the beauties of digital SLR photography and can boost the appeal of the most basic snapshot. Most of the time, a shallow depth-of-field is used to isolate a foreground subject from a distracting background but, by using a fast lens, it's possible to manipulate the blur's character for creative effect, too.

You may notice when you take a photograph with a shallow depth-of-field that the blur is made up of small circles. This effect is called 'bokeh' and is the rendition of out-of-focus points of light. With a little creativity, and a craft knife, you can change the shape of the bokeh using a self-made filter. Once you've decided what shape you want your bokeh – hearts, snowflakes, stars and half-moons work well – find a spot that has lots of separate lights as a backdrop such as a night-lit street scene, fairy lights or even dappled light through trees. A dark background makes the individual lights more prominent and you may need a tripod, as you'll most likely be shooting in low light. ➔

1 Make a bokeh filter Draw a circle onto black card to match the circumference of your lens. Do this by finding a round object of the same size or measure the diameter and use a compass. Now, draw a shape in the centre of the circle.

2 Cut out a shape Lean the card on a hard surface and then, at a 45° angle, cut the shape out using a craft or utility knife. Use scissors to cut the circle out and then secure a flap of sticky tape to the edge so you can pull the filter off the lens front with ease.

Top tips for beautiful bokeh

The wider the aperture setting, the stronger the bokeh, so start by selecting the maximum aperture of your lens. Also, play with the distance between the camera and the main subject, and the distance between the subject and the background, as this will strengthen or weaken the effect. One of the best effects can be achieved by getting as close to your subject as possible and to use selective focusing to throw the rest of the image out of focus. The size of the filter shape is also worth experimenting with, depending on the effect you want to create, because the smaller the shape, the smaller the bokeh will be. If you own a Lensbaby, try out its Creative Aperture Kit as an alternative if you don't fancy getting crafty (visit www.lensbaby.com for details).

3 Happy with the shape? If you struggle to cut out a clean shape, why not try a custom-shaped hole punch instead. And, if you don't want to risk harming the lens, how about slotting the bokeh filter onto a UV filter, or placing a square bokeh filter in a filter holder for a more reusable, sturdy version.

4 Use a macro light Stability is really important to avoid camera shake, so I rest it on the ground. I attach a macro light to illuminate the sweets, which are positioned on a piece of black card with the fairy lights behind them. You'll find that an anglepoise lamp can also be used to light the scene.

5 Remove the filter I took a frame at f/2.8 without the filter on to see how it would look without the effect added. I also noted that the black card under the sweets meant there was no separation between the bottom of the image and the background, so I switched to a shiny red card to add some interest.

6 Adjust set-up I then added the heart-shaped filter to the lens and played around with the aperture and camera-to-subject distance to see what effect it had on the bokeh. At f/5.6 and further away from the sweets, the background lights are taking shape but are by no means as large as the image taken at f/2.8.

Final image
Keeping the red card has added reflections that balance the bottom part of the frame with the top. Setting the aperture at f/2.8 and moving closer to the subjects, while playing around with the angle of the light, the focusing and the composition, gave a more dynamic shot. With a bit of tweaking to the Curves and Levels in Photoshop, I'm all done!

Still-lifes that get busy with the fizzy!

Can't get out to shoot? You can still keep your camera busy with this stay-at-home still-life technique

Ross Hoddinott: There are some days when, as much as you'd like to, you just can't leave the house. On days like these, you need a bit of inspiration to make ordinary objects more photogenic for striking still-lifes. All you need is a little imagination and creativity. If you are struggling to be inspired, though, try flicking through this magbook or issues of *Digital SLR Photography* for creative guides and stunning photography. While I'm not suggesting you copy other people's images, there is nothing wrong with adopting, adapting and improving on photographs that you see and like. This is exactly what I did one damp day when I was struggling for ideas. After a few minutes of browsing, I found a picture of drinking straws submerged in water and smothered in tiny air bubbles. The shot was simple, but had plenty of impact. It got my creative juices flowing again and a few minutes later I was creating my own unique version.

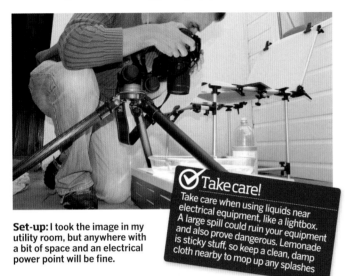

Set-up: I took the image in my utility room, but anywhere with a bit of space and an electrical power point will be fine.

✓ Take care!
Take care when using liquids near electrical equipment, like a lightbox. A large spill could ruin your equipment and also prove dangerous. Lemonade is sticky stuff, so keep a clean, damp cloth nearby to mop up any splashes

1 Ready your subject I decided to photograph pencils submerged in water. I envisaged tiny air bubbles clinging to their tips, adding scale and visual interest. I sharpened five colourful pencils so that they all had a consistent sharp tip, then taped them together.

2 Choose your backdrop When shooting still-life images, choice of background is important. Therefore, I opted for a simple, clean, white backdrop. To create this, I decided to use a lightbox. I placed it on the floor so I could easily position my tripod-mounted camera directly overhead.

3 Weigh down your subject Pencils placed in water will float away from each other, but because mine were taped together, I just had to weigh them down. I laid the pencils in a Pyrex dish, and then weighed them down with a smaller water-filled container, before submerging the pencils in water.

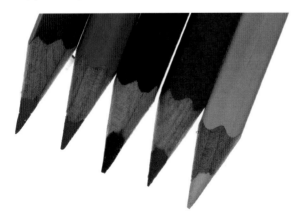

4 Take a test shot I used a macro lens to create a tight composition, but a close-up filter will also do the job. I selected an aperture of f/11 (ISO 100) and positioned the camera parallel overhead to maximise the available depth-of-field. However, the absence of air bubbles made the shot look flat.

5 Adjust your set-up Tap water obviously didn't work, so I tried lemonade instead. This had the desired effect, with hundreds of tiny air bubbles forming and clinging to the pencils. I positioned the pencils diagonally to create impact, but doing so created too much empty, wasted space.

Final image

I altered composition so that the pencils filled more of the frame. The result had far more impact. I also added a burst of fill-in flash, using the camera's built-in unit. This gave the pencils more punch and vibrancy.

Get a blooming marvellous still-life

Who knew such a simple set-up could yield such great results? Grab your torch and get shooting!

Helen Sotiriadis: Thankfully, we can explore indoor macro photography with low lighting whatever the weather, so if it's gloomy outdoors, try out this technique. All you need is a dark corner of a room, a macro lens (or any lens with a close focusing distance) and a little imagination to transform everyday household objects into works of art. There is no need for fancy lighting either – a torch is all you need.

Low-light close-up photography has its fair share of challenges. It's essential that you keep the camera absolutely still because of the long exposure times and close proximity to your subject, so it's vital that you use a tripod, along with a remote release or your DSLR's self-timer, so you don't jog the camera when releasing the shutter button. Intense contrast in your composition will also mean that you'll have to either override your camera's automatic settings, compensating the exposure by a couple of stops, or manually set the aperture and shutter speed. After the shoot, take time with a bit of strategic post-processing and you'll transform your decent shot into a striking image. ➔

Is an LED torch essential?

You may be asking yourself why we suggest you use an LED torch rather than the standard torches that can often be found. LED torches are usually far more powerful and even a small LED light can illuminate all but the largest prop. LED torches often come with a swivel head that allows the beam to be focused on a single spot or spread over a wider range. Finally, you'll notice the colour of the LED beam is much whiter than the older-type bulb torches, which helps with adjusting White Balance in post-processing.

1 Set up I lay a large sheet of black paper against a cardboard box, filled with a few books to keep it stable, for a backdrop. If space is limited, you can always lean your paper against the wall instead of a box. A sheet of dark tinted glass serves as a reflective base for your subject and also steadies the paper.

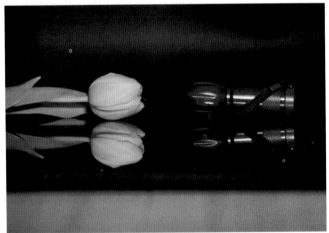

2 Set up lighting I then place an LED torch across from a beautiful white tulip so that its beam shines directly into the flower, making it appear as if it is glowing from the inside. The light also intensifies the texture of the petals. After a few test shots, consider removing any leaves if they are cluttering the composition and distracting the eye from the petals.

3 Set camera settings Keeping your camera stable on a tripod means you can lengthen the exposure time and use ISO 100 to avoid noise. As I'm shooting the tulip image in the dark with only the LED torch as a light source, it's much easier to compose and manually focus on the flower with the room lights on and then turn them off when I'm ready to shoot in the dark.

4 Adjust lighting With the room lights off, experiment with the torch's position to keep the light in the centre of the flower, illuminating the petals nearest the camera. The multi-zone metering isn't much help: here I'm using aperture-priority mode and f/2.8, giving me a shutter speed of 1/10sec, overexposing the petals and burning out its detail.

5 Fine-tune settings I switch to manual mode, keeping it set to ISO 100 and f/2.8. I start with my shutter speed at 1/10sec, and fire several shots, gradually increasing the shutter speed until the petals are properly exposed. The best results are at 1/30sec. Also experiment with the White Balance, I find the Daylight preset makes the most of the cool-blue light.

Final image

The LED light from the torch gives the impression that the tulip is glowing from within!

6 **Post-processing** Follow up with a little post-processing to enhance the texture of the petals. Use the *Polygonal Lasso Tool* in Photoshop to select the area of the flower facing the camera and *Feather* it generously to achieve a soft border to the selection. Then copy the selection onto a new *Layer* and select the *Overlay* Blend Mode to boost contrast.

7 **Crop image** I feel the composition is unbalanced in its original format and would be enhanced with a square crop, so I use the *Crop Tool* to select my new frame shape. I then use the *Spot Healing Brush Tool* to eliminate any specks of dust that inevitably appear on the reflective glass, before flattening the layers (*Layer>Flatten Image*) and saving my file.

Make a splash!

Everyone loves trying to photograph a water droplet – it's a great way to develop your high-speed timing skills

Ross Hoddinott: Water is highly photogenic, whether in large quantities or a tiny droplet. H_2O seems to be irresistible to photographers: they can 'suspend' it by using a fast shutter speed or render it as a milky blur with a lengthy exposure, capture reflections off its surface or use it to add the feeling of motion to an image. There is an infinite number of ways to shoot it, so it's no wonder that water features in so many of our images.

One picture that many photographers have a go at is a close-up of a droplet splashing into water. Yes, it is a bit of a cliché and has been done to death, but do it well and it can create a very striking image.

You don't need much room; a simple tabletop set-up in your kitchen or living room will suffice. And you only need a basic set-up: a digital camera; close-up filter or

macro lens; a single flashgun; and a handful of everyday bits and bobs. Within half an hour or so, you can be set up and ready to begin taking beautiful images of sculptured water droplets. So grab your kit and let's get started…

✓**Keep everything dry!**
It's important to keep your gear dry to prevent damage to electronics. It's worth keeping a towel handy at all times to wipe down your camera body and lens when needed

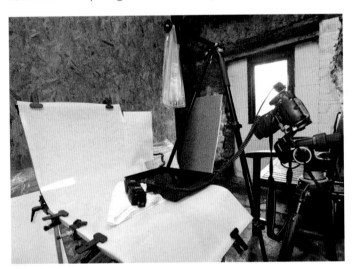

1 Set up Before you begin taking pictures, you need to arrange your set-up. You will need a container, half to three-quarters full of water, for your droplet to fall into. I used a paint tray but any large, shallow container will do. I placed this on a still-life table, but a simple tabletop set-up would do fine. Next, suspend a bag – partially full of water – 30-60cm directly overhead.

Essential kit

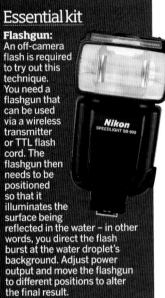

Flashgun:
An off-camera flash is required to try out this technique. You need a flashgun that can be used via a wireless transmitter or TTL flash cord. The flashgun then needs to be positioned so that it illuminates the surface being reflected in the water – in other words, you direct the flash burst at the water droplet's background. Adjust power output and move the flashgun to different positions to alter the final result.

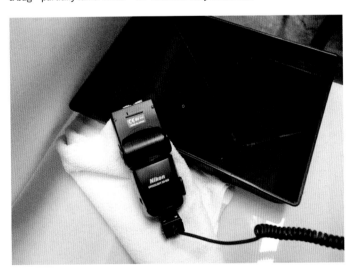

2 Consider lighting set-up I position my tripod-mounted Nikon D300 so it's shooting down into the water tray. Next, it's time to consider lighting. You need to illuminate what you see reflected in the water through the viewfinder – not the water itself. I place a sheet of white card at the end of the tray to create a simple background and angle my flashgun towards the card.

3 Set flash Now the technical bit. It's the very fast flash from the gun that effectively becomes your shutter speed, and the lower the power setting, the faster it gets. I set it to its manual mode and dial in 1/16th power to generate a fast enough speed to freeze the droplets. This is a good starting point so I recommend you use the same and make adjustments after reviewing results.

Final image
After 30 minutes, I had taken some nice images but they lacked colour, so I alter White Balance from Auto to the camera's Tungsten WB preset. Deliberately mismatching WB in this way gives my final image a blue hue.

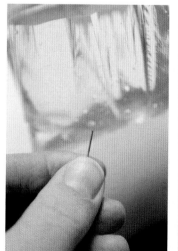

4 Manual focus I make a tiny hole in the bag using a pin to create a constant drip and hold a pencil in the water at the point where the droplets are falling to give something to focus on manually. I set an aperture of f/8 to generate enough depth-of-field to keep the droplet sharp but render ripples out of focus. I set the flash sync speed to 1/200sec and set an ISO of 200 for optimum quality.

5 Get shooting! Time to get started. Good timing and a huge slice of luck are required, so take lots of shots – hundreds possibly – to get what you are after. It is an unpredictable technique and every image is different. Expect lots of 'near misses', such as water ripples but no droplet. I found a remote release helped my timing, releasing the shutter as the droplet hit the water.

CLOSE-UP EQUIPMENT

ESSENTIAL MACRO GEAR TO HELP YOU TAKE STUNNING CLOSE-UP IMAGES

CLOSE-UP FILTERS & TUBES

MACRO LED RINGLIGHT

SPECIALIST MACRO LENSES

Close-up filters & extension tubes for £10

If you have ever wanted to get into close-up photography and capture stunning images of miniature subjects, but have always been put off by the high prices of specialist macro optics, then we're about to change your world. While dedicated macro lenses can set you back a few hundred quid, there are a number of close-up accessories that can deliver great results at a fraction of the cost. Ross Hoddinott explains…

IT'S TRUE THAT, for pure image quality and convenience, a macro lens is hard to beat. They are optimised for close focusing and available in a variety of focal lengths, ranging from 50mm to 200mm. However, they're not cheap. Macro lenses made by the likes of Sigma or Tamron cost upwards of £300 and a Canon or Nikon lens costs far more! This outlay is too high for many but, thankfully, there are other ways to get close to your subject, the most popular and cost-effective being close-up filters and extension tubes.

Close-up filters

Close-up filters (also called 'supplementary close-up lenses') screw onto the front of the lens like any other screw-in filter. They act like a magnifying glass, reducing the minimum focusing distance of a lens and allowing photographers to get closer to their subject. They're available in varying diameters to suit different filter threads. The most common sizes are 49mm, 52mm, 58mm and 67mm – remember to check which size you require before buying. They are available in a variety of strengths, typically +1, +2, +3 and +4 dioptres. The higher the number, the greater the magnification. Some brands also produce a powerful +10 version! Quite simply, there is no better, or cheaper, introduction to the fascinating world of close-up photography.

Several brands produce close-up filters, including Canon, Hoya and Nikon, and they can be bought individually or in sets. Sets usually consist of +1, +2 and +4 filters.

Shop around and you'll find good quality close-up filters for under £20. The price often varies depending on size, with smaller diameter filters being the cheapest. For the 'eBayers' among you, genuine bargains can be found. Type in the words 'close-up filter' and you will be greeted by hundreds of items. I did exactly this and, after a few moments searching, I found a set of +1, +2, +4 and +10 67mm filters from a UK seller at a 'Buy It Now' price of just £10.25, which incredibly included delivery, a filter pouch and a lifetime warranty! The set was made by Zeikos, a brand I'd not heard of before, but for £10, who cares! A few clicks later, they were ordered and arrived safely just three working days later. Find out what I thought of them on the opposite page.

Close-up filters couldn't be easier to use. They do not affect DSLR functions like metering or autofocus and do not restrict the light entering the lens, making them convenient to use handheld. It's not all good news, though. They are prone to chromatic and spherical aberration and can't match the high image quality produced by a dedicated macro lens, particularly at the edges of the frame. However, great results are possible. I actually started out using close-up filters and won my first major photo competition with an image taken using a +3 close-up filter. Quite simply, if you want to take great close-up images of texture, detail, nature and still-lifes, a close-up filter is a fantastic introduction for DSLR photographers on a budget. ➊

+4 Close-up filter

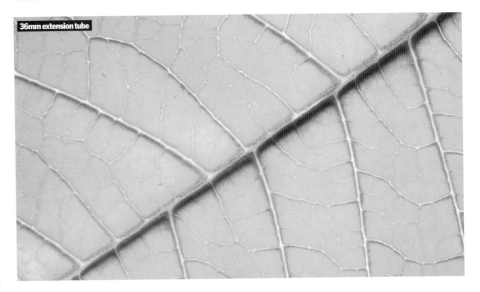

36mm extension tube

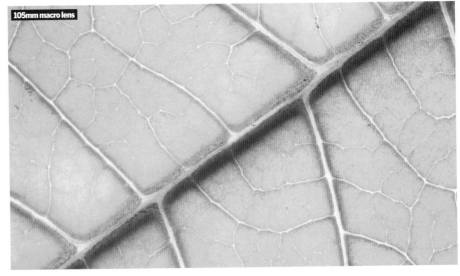

105mm macro lens

How did my £10 ebay close-up filters perform?

What can you realistically expect from a set of close-up filters costing just over ten quid? I have to be honest, my expectations weren't high when I placed my order on ebay. However, they arrived packaged well and supplied with a soft case, and my initial impressions were positive. How would they perform, though? Surely image quality would be average at best for such a small outlay? I used them in combination with a Nikon 18-70mm kit lens, which was gathering dust in my office. The great thing about close-up filters is that you simply screw them onto your lens and you're ready to shoot. I began by taking some comparison sequences to help illustrate the magnification of different strength filters. They allowed me to get much closer than the lens would focus otherwise. I avoided combining lenses together, as image quality can suffer, but the +4 filter proved powerful enough on its own, achieving a magnification of around 1:2 (half life-size) on my Nikon D300. Despite my reservations, I found image quality impressively good. Yes, it dropped toward the edges of the frame, with some colour fringing, but this is reduced at higher f/numbers, so by shooting at f/8, I kept this to a minimum. As you'd expect, image quality got progressively worse

the stronger the dioptre. However, it remained acceptable, even with the +4 filter. However, the +10 filter produced poor results. While the image centre wasn't too bad, everything else was blurry and soft. Decent +10 filters are normally expensive and constructed from two elements, so I wasn't surprised at the poor quality. However, for £10, you could chuck away the +10 filter if you wanted and just keep the +1, +2 and +4! Let's face it, a set of three close-up filters for £10 still amounts to a bargain!

+1 filter

+2 filter

+4 filter

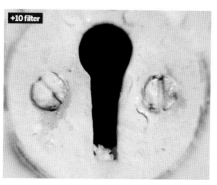
+10 filter

Tips for using close-up filters

1) You can combine close-up filters in order to further increase magnification. If you do this, attach the most powerful one first, and the weakest last. Avoid coupling three or more together as this will just exaggerate any optical flaws.

2) Close-up filters are prone to spherical aberration, which tends to soften the overall image. The effect can be minimised, though, just by selecting a higher f/number, such as f/8 or above.

3) Close-up filters can be attached to any lens, but are actually best combined with a prime focal length. The 50mm f/1.8 is an ideal lens.

Money saver!

If you own lenses with different filter threads, consider buying a 'stepping ring'. These rings adapt a filter to fit a lens with a smaller filter thread. For example, if you have a 58mm filter, but want to attach it to a 52mm thread, you could do so with the appropriate ring – saving both money and space in your camera bag. Two types of stepping rings are available – step-up and step-down. Step-up rings are the ones to go for as they are used to attach larger filters to smaller lenses; step-down rings are used for attaching smaller filters to larger lenses and run the risk of vignetting (darkening around the edges of the frame).

Popular close-up filter brands

There are a range of close-up filters on the market, ranging greatly in price. Most are of a single element construction. However, close-up filters with two elements are also available and designed to reduce the problem of chromatic aberration (colour fringing). They are more expensive, though, and you may feel you can't justify the extra expense. Listed below are some of the most commonly available close-up filters.

B+W
B+W are a renowned filter brand. They offer close-up dioptres among their range, producing +1, +2, +3, +4, +5 and +10 versions – although not all strengths are available in all filter sizes. Typically, they cost between £20 and £50 each.

Canon
Canon's close-up filters are a doublet construction – meaning two elements. They are high-quality attachments, but pricey, with larger diameter filters costing close to £150 – not exactly a budget option!

Hoya
Available in +1, +2, +3 and +4 strengths in sizes ranging from 46mm to 77mm. Hoya are a well-respected brand and a good mid-price option, with small diameter versions costing under £20 each. Recommended.

Kood
Typically, only available in a set, comprising of +1, +2 and +4 filters. They come complete with a protective case and are competitively priced, with the set costing between £20 and £50, depending on size. Definitely one for the shortlist.

Nikon
Nikon offers a limited range of high-quality but pricey filters – the 3T, 4T, 5T and 6T, along with a couple of more affordable (£45) filters (No.0 and No.1).

Zeikos
Not a familiar brand in the UK, but better known in the USA. Sold in sets of three to five strengths. They can be bought in thread sizes ranging from 52mm to 77mm and are among the cheapest available. We think they're a bargain!

Extension tubes

The other cost-effective way to get close to your subject is by using extension tubes. They are available in different camera mount fittings, and simply fit between the camera and lens in order to increase the distance between the lens and sensor. By doing so, they reduce the minimum focusing distance, allowing you to focus closer. Extension tubes are hollow; they don't contain any optical elements. This means that, unlike close-up filters, good image quality is maintained. However, they do reduce the amount of light entering the camera – the greater the magnification, the more light that is lost. Your DSLR's TTL meter automatically compensates for this, but it's worth remembering that shutter speeds will be slightly longer as a result of using one.

Extension tubes are compact, lightweight and produce excellent results. They can be bought individually or in sets of three lengths. The most common lengths are 12mm, 20mm and 36mm – the longer the tube, the closer you get, and the higher the magnification. They can also be combined together to generate high levels of magnification, equal to or even exceeding the 1:1 (life-size) capabilities of a macro lens. However, when using lots of extension, the camera-to-subject distance will be very short. This isn't a major concern for static subjects, but can prove impractical for wildlife.

Strangely, extension tubes aren't as popular today as they once were, but don't overlook them. Type in 'extension tubes' on eBay and you won't be short of choice. Remarkably, a set of three manual tubes can cost as little as a fiver, including delivery, from a UK seller. These work fine, but have no electrical contacts and as a result, exposure and focusing have to be adjusted manually. Also, to use many of them you need a lens with an aperture ring otherwise you can't adjust the f/stop. Having said that, we've tested a set of Gump extension tubes over the page, costing £7.99 including delivery, and the results surprised us. For those cameras that

lack an aperture ring, Gump tubes are supplied with a bayonet mount so that fitting is possible. We tested ours with a Canon 50mm f/1.8 – a used manual focus 50mm f/1.8 lens can be picked up for as little as £30. Therefore, you could be the proud owner of a prime lens and set of extension tubes for only £40!

If you can afford to spend more, you're better off buying a set of auto extension tubes, though, especially if you shoot moving subjects. These include electronics, which retain the camera's metering and focusing, making them the best choice. While pricier than basic tubes, they're far cheaper than a macro lens – a set of three different lengths can be had for around £100.

Get the point!
To get this frame-filling shot, a Kenko 20mm tube was used together with a 18-70mm kit lens!

> "If you can afford to spend more, you're better off with a set of auto extension tubes. While more pricey than basic tubes, they're far cheaper than a macro lens"

Extension tubes

These cost-effective, close-up attachments may not be as popular as they once were, but they are still an excellent budget option for newcomers to close-up photography. Canon, Kenko and Nikon are among the recognised brands that produce them. Cheaper versions can be easily found online on sites like eBay and Amazon. Also, look out for secondhand and discontinued versions from the likes of Teleplus and Minolta (which fit Sony DSLRs).

Canon
Canon produces both a 12mm (EF12) and 25mm (EF25) extension tube. They are compatible with EF lenses, maintaining all focus and metering connections.

Kenko
These are high-quality third-party tubes, which retain TTL exposure and focusing control. They are available in most popular camera fittings and bought in a set of 12mm, 20mm and 36mm tubes.

Nikon
Nikon produces four auto extension rings, with AI diaphragm coupling – 8mm (PK-11A), 14mm (PK-12), 27.5mm (PK-13) and 52.5mm (PN-11).

Olympus
Olympus includes the Zuiko Digital EX-25 among its accessory range. This 25mm extension tube costs in the region of £150, which is a little pricey.

Close-up ideas: What can you shoot with a close-up attachment?

1) Flowers
You can shoot great frame-filling shots of flowers, wild or cultivated, thanks to a budget close-up filter or extension tube. From amaryllis to water lilies, you'll have it covered!

2) Insects
You don't necessarily need a pricey macro to snap insects; with a close-up attachment, you have all the equipment you need to shoot stunning wildlife close-ups.

3) Still-lifes
Another popular subject that often requires a close approach, beyond the capabilities of a general day-to-day lens. Everyday subjects can look totally different in close-up.

4) Textures
An inexpensive close-up attachment will help you reveal and isolate photogenic texture, patterns and miniature detail. For example, try snapping the tip of a pencil.

Green shoots
Close-up photography allows DSLR users to isolate interesting miniature detail. You don't need a macro lens, a budget close-up attachment will suffice!

Calculating an extension tube's magnification

The magnification of an extension tube can be approximated by dividing the amount of extension by the focal length of the lens. For example, if you combine a 25mm extension tube with a 50mm lens, the reproduction ratio is 1:2 (half life-size). Using the same level of extension with a 100mm lens would result in a 1:4 (quarter life-size) reproduction. However, this represents the minimum focusing distance with the lens set to infinity – magnification increases as you focus closer.

If you wish to achieve a high level of magnification, combine them with a focal length in the region of 35mm to 70mm. Any wider than this and the camera-to-subject distance will be too short; any longer and you would need an impractical amount of extension to achieve a high level of magnification.

Other close-up accessories (they're good, but a hassle to use!)

Camera bellows
Bellows work on a similar principle to extension tubes, increasing the distance between sensor and lens for closer focusing.

Their concertina design is infinitely variable and they are capable of high magnifications. Auto bellows retain full coupling of the camera and lens, but are pricey (the Novoflex costs £400). However, search for 'bellows' on eBay, and there are budget versions available from China and Hong Kong, costing under £30 with free delivery. They are manual, so automatic functions are disabled, and you need a lens with an aperture ring in order to change f/stops. If you can pick up an old enlarging lens, this is a good choice with high optical quality, manual aperture control and, hopefully, a bargain price!

Reversing rings
Another way to magnify a subject is by reversing a lens. The lens is mounted back to front via an adaptor called a reversing ring. You need to buy a ring that fits the camera mount and also matches the filter thread of

the lens you intend using. Doing so creates a close focusing lens capable of producing high-quality results at large magnifications. To maximise image quality, it is best to only reverse prime focal lengths. However, with cheaper rings, automatic functions are lost and another adaptor may be required to keep the lens iris open. Specialist companies like Novoflex make reversing rings that retain automatic functions. The cost is similar to buying a third-party macro lens, though, so it can't be considered a budget option.

Tested: Manual extension tubes

Auto extension tubes can set you back as much as £150, but we've found an alternative that can give you good results for under a tenner!

Reviewer: Lee Frost
Product: Gump Macro Extension Tubes
Price: £7.99

Like most enthusiasts, my early days as a photographer were spent trying my hand at a range of different subjects to find out which ones got my creative juices flowing. Close-up and macro photography naturally figured, but as a cash-strapped teenager, all I could afford was a cheap reversing ring that allowed me to fit the 50mm prime lens on my Zenith SLR body back to front so that it would focus closer.

I still remember chasing insects and butterflies around the garden with this simple set-up. Talk about hard work! The only way to adjust focus was by physically moving the camera, but with depth-of-field limited to just a few millimetres, this meant that getting the right bit of the subject in focus was almost impossible – especially when handholding the camera or shooting in windy weather! How I managed not to throw my camera over the neighbour's hedge I'll never know, but I did realise very quickly that macro photography wasn't for me and promptly settled on landscapes!

Fast-forward 30 years and when editor Lezano asked me if I fancied testing a set of extension tubes for *Digital SLR Photography* magazine's *Budget Photo* feature, I could feel the muscles in my neck tighten. Clearly, I still hadn't recovered from the trauma of those past macro experiences, but it's a well-documented fact that the only way to conquer fear is by facing it head-on, so like an arachnophobe about to stick his head in a box of spiders, I swallowed a couple of paracetamol, took a deep breath and agreed!

Extension tubes have been around for decades. They're basically hollow tubes that fit between the camera body and lens, allowing the lens to focus much closer – the more extension you use, the greater the magnification and

closer the focus. The rule of thumb is that if the amount of extension in millimetres matches the effective focal length of the lens, a reproduction ratio of life-size is achieved. So, if you use a 50mm tube with a 50mm lens/focal length you'll get life-size (1:1) repro, which in real terms means you can fill the frame with an area the same size as the camera's sensor – 24x36mm in the case of a full-frame DSLR.

Camera manufacturers tend to offer tubes in single units and different sizes, so you can buy one or more as required. Independent manufacturers usually make extension tubes in sets of three, each a different size. In either case you can use a single tube or combine them to achieve greater magnification.

Compared to the cost of a bellows unit (not so popular now) or a pukka macro lens, extension tubes have always offered a cut-price route into macro photography – relatively speaking. For example, a Canon Extension Tube EF25II will set you back around £150, while a set of three Kenko tubes costs about the same, compared to £700 or so for a Canon EF 100mm f/2.8 Macro IS USM lens. That's a big difference in price, but nothing compared to the £7.99 we paid for the set of Gump Macro Extension Tubes we're trying out here – and if you shop around, you may even find other brands for less!

Essentially, these budget tube sets are the same as the more expensive ones and do the same job. The main difference, and the reason why the price tags are so radically different, is that the pricey models have electronic links to retain exposure and autofocus, whereas the cheaper ones are fully manual. In other words, there's no linkage between camera and lens, so you have to use manual exposure and focus.

DID YOU KNOW?
If you can't stretch to £7.99 for a set of Gump extension tubes, try making your own using the cardboard tube from the middle of a roll of loo paper! Paint it black inside and attach your camera and lens using tape.

For you autofocus diehards out there, this may seem like too much of a step back to contemplate. However, the reality is that experienced macro photographers tend to focus manually even when using autofocus gear. Why? Because depth-of-field is extremely limited at close focusing distances, so accurate focusing on exactly the right spot is crucial. That's easier to do by relying on hand and eye rather than technology.

Considering the cost, first impressions of the Gump tubes were very positive. For your £7.99 (including postage) you get five 'bits' – a Canon EF bayonet mount that allows you to connect the tubes to your Canon DSLR, three tubes measuring 9mm, 16mm and 30mm, plus a further Canon EF mount to accept your Canon-fit lens. Each item connects to the next via a screw thread, and mounts are available for other camera makes, so if you switch from Canon to Nikon, say, you can buy the necessary bits to make the tubes compatible. Though with such a low price tag, you might as well just buy a complete set of new tubes with the relevant mounts.

As already mentioned, you can use each tube individually by screwing the body and lens mounts to either end, or combine any two, or use all three. I tried every combination possible and fitted my trusty Canon EF 50mm f/1.8 to the end. I paid under £80 for this cracking lens, and combined with the £7.99 for the tubes, it gives me a fantastic macro set-up capable of ➔

£7.99

Gump Macro Extension Tubes

Guide price: £7.99 (inc postage)

Fit: All Canon EOS EF/EF-S DSLRs

Operation: Manual focus, manual exposure, manual aperture stopdown

Construction: Metal

Weight: 112g

In the box: Body mount, 9mm, 16mm, 30mm tubes and bayonet lens mount

We purchased this set of extension tubes from www.amazon.co.uk and if the fantastic price wasn't enough, they were delivered for free and arrived in just two days! There are other budget extension tube sets available at Amazon and elsewhere, from brands such as BV and Jo, Fotodix, Neewer and Power Planet. They all do the same job and in some cases may well have originated from the same factory! Our set was for Canon EOS cameras only, but you can buy sets to fit Nikon and other DSLR brands.

Above: If you're patient and take your time, it's possible to produce stunning close-ups using the Gump tubes.

Top left: Ideally, mount your camera on a tripod when using the extension tubes so you can avoid camera shake.

Comparison set: This comparison of a US dollar banknote shows just how powerful the tubes are and how close you can focus to fill the frame with a very small area.

50mm lens

9mm tube

16mm tube

30mm tube

All three tubes

Auto vs manual tubes

Automatic and manual extension tubes look virtually identical, do exactly the same job and produce images of comparable quality – but there are significant differences, as outlined below.

MANUAL EXTENSION TUBES

The clue is in the name – they lack any kind of automated operation. You need to set your camera to manual exposure mode and though the TTL metering system may give a fairly accurate exposure, be prepared to override it. When it comes to focusing, it's manual all the way and you need to focus very carefully. Using any aperture other than the widest is a fiddle but doable – see over the page.

- ✓ Fantastic value for money
- ✓ High image quality
- ✓ Lightweight and compact
- ✗ Slow and fiddly to use
- ✗ Viewfinder image is very dark
- ✗ Unsuitable for 'wildlife' close-ups

AUTOMATIC EXTENSION TUBES

If you're willing to pay about 20x more than the Gump ones cost for a set of tubes, you get full linkage with your DSLR's electronics, so you can use the TTL metering system and should get accurate results. You can also select any f/number and benefit from auto aperture stopdown when you trip the shutter and the lens's AF system will work. That said, manual focus might still be preferable.

- ✓ Quicker and easier to use
- ✓ High image quality
- ✓ Better build quality
- ✗ Viewfinder image is still very dark
- ✗ Significantly more expensive
- ✗ Manual focus preferable to AF

Close encounters: The Gump extension tubes allow you to produce interesting images of all kinds of natural and man-made objects, from plants and mushrooms to cutlery and sweets! These images only scratch the surface of what's possible with this close-up bargain.

life-size repro for under £90. Music to the ears of a tight northerner.

To put the tubes through their paces, I started out by shooting some close-ups of a colourful gerbera. Ideally, I would have gone outside where light levels were higher, but a strong breeze put a stop to that idea with the slightest bit of subject movement making it very difficult to focus due to a distinct lack of depth-of-field.

The solution was to move indoors where there was no breeze, but as light levels were lower, this led to another problem. The more extension you use, the darker the viewfinder image gets. Not only that, increased extension also means that depth-of-field is more limited, which makes critical focusing essential, but more difficult to achieve because you can't see what you're focusing on! I tried using LiveView on my EOS 5D Mk II, but couldn't see the

subject clearly and in the end resorted to shining a torch on the flower so I could see it enough to focus. I would then take a test shot, enlarge it on the preview screen to check sharpness, and if it wasn't quite there, I would move the flower fractionally closer to or further away from the camera and take another shot. This proved to be quite a laborious process, but it worked and resulted in great images, so it was well worth it.

A further factor to consider when using manual tubes is that you can't adjust the lens aperture as normal because nothing happens – it stays set at the widest (maximum) aperture, which in the case of my 50mm lens is f/1.8. Depth-of-field is pretty shallow at f/1.8 when using the lens normally, but stick a set of extension tubes between it and the camera body and it becomes almost non-existent.

There is a fiddly solution to this problem when using Canon DSLRs (see panel, opposite) and I used it to take some shots with the lens stopped all the way down to f/22 to maximise depth-of-field (maximise being a relative term as it was still only a few millimetres!). Unfortunately, as this involves stopping the lens down manually before taking the shot, the viewfinder image becomes even darker, and indoors, exposure times become inordinately long – up to 25 seconds in some cases with the shots I took. Not a problem with the camera on a sturdy tripod, the subject absolutely still and the shutter fired with a remote release, but clearly not suitable for anything that can move.

When it comes to determining correct exposure, a little experimentation is required. You can't simply set your camera to aperture-priority and fire away – shooting in manual mode is a necessity. I would take a test shot at a guesstimated shutter speed, check the image and histogram then adjust the shutter speed accordingly and retake. It usually took two or three attempts to get the exposure spot-on, after which it was plain sailing.

Over the course of an afternoon, I took dozens of shots and gradually got into the swing of it.

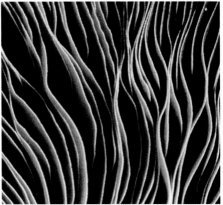

Having worked indoors in available light with the camera on a tripod, I moved outdoors with just the smallest tube fitted and took some handheld shots of plants in my garden with the aperture set to a modest f/8 and the ISO increased to 400. Extension tubes cause a light loss that requires the exposure to be increased, just like some filters do, so I found that a higher ISO rating was necessary to maintain a decent shutter speed of 1/100sec or faster. When I got it right, image sharpness was surprisingly high.

Achieving sharp focus was best done by gently moving the camera closer to or further away from the subject, then quickly firing when the desired area came into focus. Repeating this process several times ensured I got one shot just right, and slight changes to the sharp focus zone resulted in widely different images. I actually enjoyed playing with the lack of depth-of-field as I ended up taking a lot of shots at a wide aperture so only a tiny sliver of the subject came out sharp while everything else faded to a soft blur.

I can't imagine that macro-maestro Ross Hoddinott will be rushing out to buy a set of Gump tubes, and if you fancy shooting close-ups of the kind of critters he tends to stalk you'll probably end up chucking yours in the nearest pond out of sheer frustration. They're not designed for handheld use or for subjects that are likely to move around. But if you're sticking to static subjects in a relatively controlled environment, as I did, and you take your time and learn from your mistakes, they're capable of fantastic results.

For £7.99, they represent the best photographic bargain I've come across in my entire career.

Canon's DOF preview

As already mentioned, a big drawback with manual extension tubes is that you can't adjust the lens aperture in the normal way due to the lack of electronic linkage between camera and lens. This technically limits you to shooting only with the lens at its maximum/widest aperture, but in the case of Canon EOS DSLRs, there is a trick you can employ to set smaller apertures:

1) With the lens mounted directly to the camera body, set the aperture you want – f/8 f/11, f/16 or whatever.

2) Depress the depth-of-field (DOF) preview button on the camera body so the diaphragm in the lens stops down to the aperture selected.

3) While holding down the DOF preview button, remove the lens and you'll find the aperture remains stopped down.

4) Fit the extension tubes to the camera then the lens to the extension tubes and prepare to take your shots with the lens preset to the selected aperture.

This is a fiddly process to go through each time you want to change aperture. Also, once you stop down beyond f/8 the viewfinder image starts to get very dark – at f/16 or f/22 you really need to be in strong light in order to see clearly enough to focus, or shine a torch on your subject to aid focus. You can try using LiveView, but it still gives a dark image.

If you use Nikon or Pentax and have older series lenses with aperture rings on the barrel, you can focus with the lens wide open, then set the aperture you want to use on the ring before firing the shutter.

Tested: Macro LED ringlight

For less than £30, you can equip yourself with a macro LED ringlight. It ain't bad, either. Let's take a look…

Reviewer: Daniel Lezano
Product: Ring 48 Macro LED
Price: £28

A ringlight is a relatively new innovation in the world of photography. It looks much like the ringflash units that have long been used by close-up enthusiasts and attach the same way – via the lens's filter thread. While its purpose is also to illuminate nearby subjects, it has a number of notable differences to ringflash (see panel over the page), the main one being the lights remain constantly on, rather than flashing at the moment of exposure. This is because rather than housing flash tubes, the ringlight is fitted with several small white LED lights, much like you'll find in pocket torches. These produce a cleaner, brighter light than the traditional light bulb, while also consuming less power and lasting far longer. They're also relatively inexpensive to produce, which is why LED torches can be picked up from a DIY store for £1 and why ringlights sporting 48 of the bright little blighters can be bought for under £30.

Whether or not these budget lights are worth investing in is what this article sets out to discover. With dedicated ringflashes costing well into three figures, you could be in for a substantial saving if our Ring 48 unit proves to be a star performer.

We ordered our unit from Amazon and were pleased to find it was delivered to our door within a couple of days. Costing less than £30, you'd be forgiven for thinking this is the most basic of lights but, in truth, it has more than you may have bargained for. For your £28 (including delivery!), your kit contains the ringlight, the hotshoe-mounted power controller, a mains plug and six adaptor rings that allow you to fit the ringlight to lenses with filter threads ranging from 49mm to 67mm.

You've two options when it comes to power – you can use two AA alkaline or rechargeable batteries when out and about, or when indoors switch to using the supplied three-volt mains adaptor instead if you so wish. This isn't a bad choice – looking around at other models, many use battery power only.

The ringlight is made up of 48 small white LED lights, which remain constantly lit – in other words, there is no option to use them as a flash. Your only control of the light output is a switch on the side, which allows you to have all 48 LEDs lit, the 24 on the left side of the ring, or the 24 on the right side.

The power controller is a unit that is attached to the camera via the hotshoe mount. On one side are two sockets – an Output socket at the top that connects to the ringlight and the DC-in socket that connects to the mains power via the supplied adaptor. On the opposite side is the on/off switch that also selects between battery and mains power, with a red light that illuminates while the unit remains switched on.

Compared to the better-known marque ringflash units, our Ring 48 model is very basic. The Canon MR-14EX, for example, boasts twin modelling lamps and flash, a far higher power setting, E-TTL wireless autoflash and an

Above: My choice of outfit for this test was the Canon EOS 550D with Tamron 60mm f/2 macro lens. The Ring 48 attaches to the front via the 55mm ring.

Right: A gerbera with a green ring binder behind it was well-lit by the LED ringlight.

DID YOU KNOW?
Dedicated ringflash units cost well into three figures, so an LED ringlight is a far more affordable lighting option for close-ups!

illuminated LCD panel to make it far easier to use. You prefer one of these, do you? Then feel free to part with £460 and be on your merry way…

Decided to hang around now to learn more about the Ring 48? Good. Then let's carry on and find out just what is possible (and what isn't!) with our budget-priced mail-order ringlight.

The primary purpose of this type of light is for use in close-ups and that's where we'll be focusing our attention in this article. However, as the sales blurb and instructions state, the Ring 48 is also suitable for portraits. I was very dubious about this statement, to be honest – as I assumed the low power of the unit would mean you would need to be within close to the subject to provide sufficient illumination and at this close range, 48 LED lights are sure to prove very uncomfortable for the subject. However, in the interest of editorial integrity, I decided that before using it for close-ups, I'd give it a try

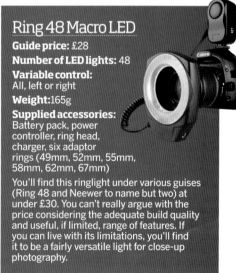

Ring 48 Macro LED

Guide price: £28
Number of LED lights: 48
Variable control: All, left or right
Weight: 165g
Supplied accessories: Battery pack, power controller, ring head, charger, six adaptor rings (49mm, 52mm, 55mm, 58mm, 62mm, 67mm)

You'll find this ringlight under various guises (Ring 48 and Neewer to name but two) at under £30. You can't really argue with the price considering the adequate build quality and useful, if limited, range of features. If you can live with its limitations, you'll find it to be a fairly versatile light for close-up photography.

shooting a head and shoulders portrait.

For all the images, I set the camera to aperture-priority mode at f/4 with the ISO rating set at 400. I'd then make adjustments to both to ensure the shutter speeds avoided shake and to vary depth-of-field. ➔

Macro: ringlight v ringflash

A macro ringlight and macro ringflash are fairly similar, but they do have some major differences. We've outlined the main ones below, along with the advantages and disadvantages of each type of lighting.

Macro ringlight

These use a set of bright LED lights that are arranged in a similar housing to a ringflash. The main difference to a flash is the lights are on permanently, which limits their working range and drains batteries. They offer some basic lighting control. Most are daylight-balanced.

- ✔ Very affordable
- ✔ Fairly versatile
- ✔ Battery & mains power
- ✗ Limited range
- ✗ Limited lighting control
- ✗ Too harsh for high-quality portraits

Macro ringflash

As its name suggests, this pumps out a flash burst when you press the shutter, with TTL flash control ensuring accurate exposures. Modelling lights are used to aid focus and most allow a degree of lighting control. For subtle lighting and ultimate control, it's the best choice.

- ✔ Sophisticated lighting control
- ✔ More powerful than ringlights
- ✗ Far more expensive

For the portraits, I enlisted team member Donna to sit in the studio and face the prospect of 48 LED lights at close quarters. As it turned out, the brightness of the LEDs was better than expected, meaning I could shoot from a reasonable distance and still capture a head and shoulders portrait while handholding the camera. Therefore, while bright, I was able to take a number of frames before the lights proved too dazzling. As for the results? Well, they were better than expected and not too far off what you could achieve with a ringflash adaptor like the Orbis or RayFlash.

I used the excellent Tamron 60mm f/2 macro lens for the portraits and close-up images in this article. With an effective focal length of 96mm on my Canon EOS 550D, it was ideal for portraits as well as macro.

With the portrait test out of the way, it was time to concentrate on the primary use of the ringlight: close-up photography. Unfortunately, the wet weather meant I wasn't able to try the ringlight out in the garden, so had to concentrate on indoor subjects, primarily flowers. However, this restriction on subject matter forced me into looking for creative ways of shooting my subjects to provide enough variety to the images.

I started off by taking a straightforward picture of a small gerbera. With the ringlight attached to the Tamron lens, the lighting from the ringlight proved shadowless as expected, making it ideal for capturing some abstract images of its petals. As well as using different viewpoints and apertures, I also tried changing the colour of the backgrounds, using nothing more fancy than coloured ring binders! I then used a similar set-up to shoot some images of a rose but from further away.

Way back in autumn, I collected a number of brown and red leaves for future use in still-lifes. They've sat in a box under my desk since then, but at long last, I had my opportunity to photograph them. My first attempts of shooting the leaves weren't great, with the dry textures of

Top left: Portraits are possible although the harsh, bright light from the LEDs aren't ideal!

Top right: Shooting a rose from further away slightly reduces the harshness of the LED lights.

Above: I placed the ringlight behind the leaves to reveal their intricate structure and colour.

the leaves not being particularly photogenic. So instead, I took the ringlight off the lens and placed it on the floor facing the camera, then placed a leaf in the space between so that the light shone through it. The backlit effect through the translucent leaf gave far more striking results, especially when using two different coloured leaves in the image.

Having done this, I discovered that using the ringlight off-camera really opens up the picture-taking possibilities. Regretfully, I didn't have enough time to try out a few of my ideas, including shooting jewellery with the ringlight directly above or backlighting a sheet of white

LED ringlight: Top tips

Use the following tips to help you take better pictures with your LED ringlight

1) Set your camera to aperture-priority
Select the aperture you want to use and keep an eye on the shutter speed – increase the ISO rating if shake is a risk.

2) Make sure you switch it off!
There is no safety shut-off, so switch the power unit off to preserve battery life.

3) Watch out for reflective subjects
Metallic objects cause strong hotspots.

4) Use mains power whenever possible
Plugging the ringlight into the mains may seem inconvenient, but it means you don't have to worry about draining batteries.

5) Experiment with reflectors
Use a handheld reflector to help shape the ringlight's output to improve results.

6) Keep spare batteries handy!
A fresh set of AAs only manages between 1-2 hours, so ensure you have spares.

7) Use the ringlight off the lens!
Get creative with lighting by using the ringlight behind or to the side of the subject.

paper and placing flowers, ferns and thistles in front to create silhouettes.

However, in the time I did have to use it, I was left in no doubt that if you're willing to experiment a little, you'll find this budget ringlight to be a brilliant aid to your close-up photography – for that, it comes highly recommended.

Autumn colour
You don't have to leave the
ringlight attached to the
lens – in fact, taking it off
opens up far more options
for creative lighting!

Tamron SP AF 60mm f/2 Di II LCD Macro

Guide price: £490	
Street price: £370	
Construction: 14 elements in ten groups	
Maximum aperture: f/2	
Minimum aperture: f/22	
Filter thread: 55mm	
Angle of view (APS-C): 26° (diagonally)	
No. of diaphragm blades: Seven	
Minimum focus: 23cm	
Maximum magnification ratio: 1:1 (life-size)	
Dimensions: 73x80mm	
Weight: 400g	
Supplied accessory: Hood	
Fittings: Canon, Nikon and Sony (APS-C only)	
Contact: www.intro2020.com	

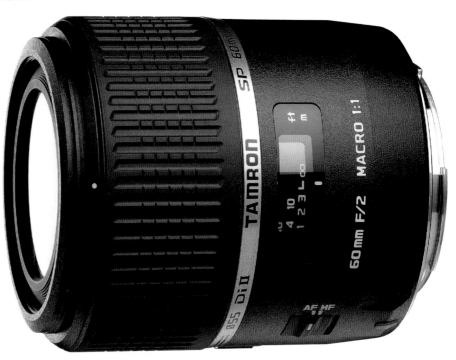

TAMRON HAS LONG ENJOYED a reputation for producing some of the finest macro lenses, including the classic 90mm f/2.8 and new VC version (opposite). This 60mm f/2 lens first appeared in 2009 and scored a Best Buy in *Digital SLR Photography* magazine's October issue that year. Since then, we've used the lens for much of our close-up work to provide a more rounded view of its handling and performance.

This lens sits alongside the two 90mm f/2.8 macros and 180mm f/3.5 in the Tamron range, giving close-up enthusiasts excellent choice. Unlike the other Tamron macros, this is part of the Di II range, suitable only for use with APS-C sensors. We used the Tamron on the Canon EOS 550D and EOS 650D, giving an effective focal length of 96mm. The other key difference (and advantage) of the 60mm lens over the other Tamrons, and indeed every other macro lens, is its very fast maximum aperture of f/2, which gives it a full stop advantage over its f/2.8 rivals. The key benefits are a brighter viewfinder, the ability to shoot handheld in low light without needing to raise the ISO rating and the extremely shallow depth-of-field. While you may not always want depth-of-field to be exploited with close-ups, where it's usually at a premium, it can be useful when shooting portraits.

The small size of the lens is impressive given the wide maximum aperture and along with the light weight makes it a lovely lens to handle. The grooved texture makes it easy to use manual focus when needed. To use manual rather than autofocus, you can rotate the lens while still in AF to make one-off adjustments or switch the lens to MF to leave it permanently in manual.

The AF is a little louder than the likes of the Canon USM and Nikon AF-S systems, but that isn't a real issue. In terms of speed and response, it is very good whether shooting close-ups or when used for everyday subjects like portraits. There is some hunting at very short distances, but this is expected and can be reduced by using the central point only.

This lens offers life-size reproduction allowing it to be used at the widest aperture for creative abstracts. The optics include two low-dispersion glass elements to improve sharpness and minimise aberrations, while anti-reflection coatings counteract glare and ghosting.

The net result of Tamron's macro heritage and latest innovations is a razor-sharp lens that reveals minute detail in the subject. The shallow depth-of-field at maximum aperture is incredible for isolating a small part of the subject and is a real creative tool. Shop around and you'll find the Tamron for around £370, with the Canon EF-S 60mm f/2.8 USM Macro a similar price and the Nikon 60mm f/2.8G ED AF-S Micro around £50 more. Considering its faster aperture and similar optical quality, this makes the Tamron excellent value for money and a deserved Best Buy.

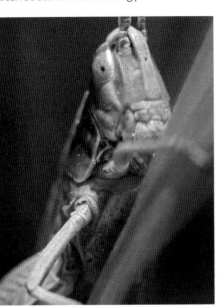

Above: Taken while testing the Canon EOS 650D, the Tamron optic delivers first-rate results.

Right: The very fast maximum aperture allows you to minimise depth-of-field.

Verdict

Longer focal lengths like the 90mm and 105mm macro lenses offer the benefit of a longer working distance, so if you're shooting insects and other forms of wildlife you're less likely to frighten them away, while also being less likely to obscure the light falling on the scene. However, you need to balance this with the benefits this lens provides, namely the faster maximum aperture, the more compact, lightweight package and the lower price. If these latter factors appeal most, you'll find the Tamron SP AF 60mm f/2 Di II lens to be a superb optic for shooting high-quality close-ups.

BEST BUY — Digital SLR Photography

Handling	★★★★★
Features	★★★★☆
Performance	★★★★★
Value	★★★★★
OVERALL	★★★★★

Tamron SP AF 90mm f/2.8 Di VC USD Macro

Guide price:	£920
Street price:	£625
Construction:	14 elements in 11 groups
Maximum aperture:	f/2.8
Minimum aperture:	f/32
Filter thread:	58mm
Angle of view:	27° (diagonally, on full-frame)
No. of diaphragm blades:	Nine
Minimum focus:	30cm
Maximum magnification ratio:	1:1 (life-size)
Dimensions:	76.4x122.9mm
Weight:	550g
Supplied accessory:	Hood
Fittings:	Canon, Nikon & Sony (APS-C & full-frame)
Contact:	www.intro2020.com

WITH A WEALTH OF affordable close-up accessories on the market, more people than ever can savour the wonders of the miniature world. However, as good as these accessories are, they can't match the convenience, ease of use and performance of a dedicated macro lens. Designed for use primarily at very short focusing distances to give very high magnification results, the macro lens is a favourite in nature photography.

Tamron's 90mm lens has seen several incarnations over the years and each has become a classic in its own right. It has remained one of the most popular macro lenses ever since the original manual focus lens was introduced in 1979. This version offers life-size reproduction and is for use with full-frame and APS-C DSLRs. It boasts a new optical design, improved AF and, for the first time, Image Stabilisation, making it one of the best-specified macro lenses at this focal length.

The Tamron boasts a longer working distance than 50mm and 60mm lenses, but shorter than the 150mm and 180mm lenses, used predominantly by pro macro photographers. In many respects it's an ideal focal length for enthusiasts, providing a decent working distance (making it less likely to obstruct light or

Above: The Tamron 90mm offers a performance comparable to marque lenses. This snowdrop was taken at a very wide aperture in order to isolate it from the background.

frighten flighty creatures) and making it suitable as a short telephoto (perfect for portraits). It's worth noting its effective focal length with APS-C DSLRs is 135mm (Nikon and Sony) or 144mm (Canon).

The Tamron optics include two XLD (Extra Low Dispersion) glass elements and one LD (Low Dispersion) element to minimise aberrations, while a rounded diaphragm promises to produce stunning bokeh. To increase the odds of sharp results when shooting handheld or in low light, Vibration Compensation is incorporated into the design, with a claimed benefit of three to four stops. To improve image quality further, the 90mm benefits from eBAND (Extended Bandwidth & Angular-Dependency), which is Tamron's latest multi-coating technology, promising to minimise flare and ghosting.

The Tamron 90mm is the latest to feature USD (Ultrasonic Silent Drive) for very fast and quiet AF. The internal focusing system means the lens barrel doesn't rotate or change length while focusing. Full-time manual focus allows you to focus manually without needing to switch from AF to manual.

The lens is designed well, with a very wide rubberised focus ring at the front that covers close to half the barrel length. A focus window displays distances in metres and feet, along with the reproduction ratio. The lens is quite lightweight but feels very well made and balances nicely in the hand. While it doesn't feel as solid as Canon or Nikon macro lenses, it feels tough nonetheless.

We used our Tamron lens on a Canon EOS 650D and found the AF to be near-silent, fast and positive. It hunts at times at very close focusing distances but this is the case with all macro lenses. Manual focus can be engaged without switching off AF, which is ideal when you want to make fine adjustments. When AF

Other popular macro lenses

Nikon AF-S VR 105mm f/2.8G IF ED Micro
Guide price: £782
Street price: £629
Robust build, Vibration Reduction and incredible optics has made this a popular lens with professionals.

Canon EF 100mm f/2.8L Macro IS USM
Guide price: £1,060
Street price: £700
Superb optics and Image Stabilisation. Canon also has another 100mm f/2.8 macro for around £450 (without IS).

Sigma 105mm f/2.8 EX OS HSM
Guide price: £700
Street price: £550
Sigma updates its acclaimed medium-tele macro with Optical Stabilisation and HSM focus. Great lens with brilliant optics.

struggles, switch from AF to M and you'll find the focus ring provides a smooth action.

In terms of image quality, the Tamron delivers first-rate results. Sharpness is very good when wide open and excellent once you stop down to mid-settings, with f/8 and f/11 capturing superb detail. Flare is very well controlled, distortion non-existent and contrast and colour fidelity is excellent. There is light fall-off of around 1.5 stops at the corners with the lens wide open, but this is normal with fast optics, so of little concern. Our tests of the stabiliser found we could capture sharp images at 1/15sec handheld, so you can expect up to three stops of benefit at close focusing distances.

Overall, the Tamron produces an excellent performance in every department. Its guide price makes it more expensive than marque rivals, but the street price around £650 is far more appropriate and proves excellent value.

Verdict

Fans of the Tamron 90mm won't be disappointed with this latest version. The addition of USD focusing and Vibration Compensation are very welcome, but it's the optical performance that stands out. The use of XLD and LD glass, along with eBAND multi-coating, really makes a difference, delivering images that will satisfy enthusiasts and pros alike. The only real negative is the high suggested guide price of £920, which is more expensive than marque optics, but the lens will sell for much less. If you are looking for a premium macro lens and can find it for around £625, then the Tamron is a great buy.

Digital SLR Photography BEST BUY

Handling	★★★★☆
Features	★★★★★
Performance	★★★★★
Value	★★★★☆
OVERALL	★★★★☆

Be sure to bracket!
Whether you use the grey card or not, in tricky lighting conditions, bracket your exposure by +/-1 stops using your camera's exposure compensation or AEB functions to ensure a correct exposure

Metered to perfection!
Scenes with strong backlighting can lead to exposure error. Use a grey card and you should have no problems.

How to use your metering & White Balance cards

The 18% grey card can be used to ensure perfect exposures when you're shooting in tricky lighting conditions. Both reference cards can also be used to set a custom White Balance, but how you do this depends on your camera (refer to your camera's manual). In the meantime, here is a brief explanation to get you started

DIGITAL CAMERAS USE sophisticated exposure systems with a choice of metering patterns to suit different lighting situations. The systems work on the assumption that the area of the scene being metered is a mid-tone, or 18% grey to be precise; the average if all dark, light and mid-tones were mixed together. It's the basis of all metering patterns and works surprisingly well, but can render incorrect exposures when the overall scene or subject is considerably lighter or darker than 18% grey. For example, very dark areas can fool the metering system into overexposing the image, while very light areas can fool the camera into underexposure, as the light meter will take a reading that renders it as a mid-tone.

As a camera is trying to render an image 'grey', it's your job to ensure you compensate to keep the tones true to life. You can do this by either using one of your camera's exposure override facilities, such as exposure compensation, the AE-Lock button or by metering from an area of the

scene that has a mid-tone. And that's where our grey card comes in. Using it is very simple as our step-by-step guide below illustrates.

The key thing to remember is that you need to place the grey card in similar lighting to your subject, for instance, don't place it in a shaded area if your subject is bathed in sunlight. Also, make sure that the card fills the metering area – we would recommend you use spot or partial metering as the card won't need to fill the entire image area – but any is suitable. You can either lock the exposure using your camera's AE-Lock facility or note the aperture and shutter speed, then switch to manual mode and dial in these settings. This latter method isn't suitable on days where lighting is variable. The card has AF reference lines to help your camera's autofocus lock on to it. However, you don't necessarily need it to be in focus to work correctly. The grey card (as well as the white card) can also be used to take a custom White Balance reading from, too.

1 Getting started If shooting in difficult lighting conditions, such as capturing a backlit subject, place the grey card in the location under the same lighting as your subject and angle it towards you.

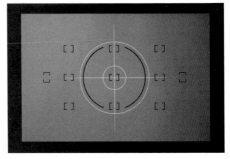

2 Take a meter reading Ensure that the entire metering area is filled by the grey card (in this instance we're using spot metering) and lock the exposure with the AE-Lock button.

3 Compose & shoot With this exposure locked, you can compose your scene and take your shots. When you check it on your LCD monitor, the exposure should be perfect.